RR TEST PREP

DIGITAL SAT®

FULL-LENGTH PRACTICE TEST

RAMANA RAO MLV

RAGHAVENDER J.

CONTENTS

READING AND WRITING MODULE 1

33 Questions

Directions: The questions in this section address a number of important reading and writing skills. Each question includes one or more passages, which may include a table or graph. Read each passage and question carefully, and then choose the best answer to the question based on the passage(s). All questions in this section are multiple-choice with four answer choices. Each question has a single best answer.

Question 1

Brown University, a private Ivy League research university in Providence, Rhode Island, was established in 1764. At the time of its creation, Brown's charter was uniquely _____; while other colleges had curricular strictures against opposing doctrines, Brown's charter asserted, "Sectarian differences of opinions shall not make any Part of the Public and Classical instruction."

Which choice completes the text with the most logical and precise word or phrase?

    A) orthodox
    B) proverbial
    C) progressive
    D) controversial

Question 2

Spanish flue is a common misnomer for the 1918 flue pandemic whose fatality was estimated at 6 to 10 million in the United States alone. The pandemic broke out near the end of World War I, when wartime censors in belligerent countries suppressed bad news to maintain morale, but newspapers freely reported the outbreak in neutral Spain, creating _____ impression of Spain as the epicenter of the disease.

Which choice completes the text with the most logical and precise word or phrase?

    A) a false
    B) a threatening
    C) a realistic
    D) an unbiased

Question 3

Electroluminescence (the process of releasing light from electrons) from single molecules that form a thin layer on a semi-conductor imposes _____ demands for molecule-electrode coupling. To conduct electrons, the molecular orbitals need to be hybridized with electrodes. To emit light, they need to be decoupled from the electrodes to prevent the absorption of fluorescence.

Which choice completes the text with the most logical and precise word or phrase?

A) persistent
B) consequential
C) transient
D) inconsistent

Question 4

In 1784, some 130 years before Einstein proposed black holes, English astronomical pioneer John Michell _____ the existence of black holes, bodies so big that even light could not escape from them. Michell's wild guess depended on simplistic calculations that assumed that such a body might have the same density of the Sun. his calculations also concluded that 'dark star' would form when its diameter exceeds the Sun's by a factor of 500, making the star extremely small.

Which choice completes the text with the most logical and precise word or phrase?

A) established
B) refuted
C) recanted
D) surmised

Question 5

Based on her own experiences and her study of Native American cultures, Paula Gunn Allen wrote *The Sacred Hoop: Recovering the Feminine in American Indian Traditions* (1986). This ground-breaking work argued that the dominant cultural view of Native American societies was biased and that European explorers understood Native Peoples through the patriarchal lens. She _____ such views by describing the central role women played in many Native American cultures.

Which choice completes the text with the most logical and precise word or phrase?

A) underscored
B) undermined
C) protested
D) proclaimed

Question 6

By definition, parasites are costly for their hosts as they _____ resources for their own growth, reproduction, and survival with no rewards for the hosts. Given the cost of parasitism, hosts are expected to evolve defense mechanisms aiming at limiting the negative effect of parasitism on their fitness. Consequently, hosts have evolved a series of morphological, physiological and behavioral adaptations to fight off parasitic attacks.

Which choice completes the text with the most logical and precise word or phrase?

A) squander
B) divert
C) optimize
D) manage

Question 7

In the early 1960s, American computer scientist Paul Baran developed the concept that he called 'distributed adaptive message block switching', with a goal of providing 'safe' method for telecommunication of messages. His ideas contradicted the then-established principles of pre-allocation of network bandwidth, exemplified by the development of telecommunications in the Bell system. The new concept found little resonance among network implementers until the independent work of British computer scientist Donald Davies in 1965. Davies was credited with coining the modern term *packet switching*, a concept leading to development of ARPANET, the precursor network of the modern internet.

Which choice best states the main purpose of the text?

A) To bring out fundamental differences between two communication systems

B) To contrast the works of two computer scientists

C) To describe how the work of two scientists helped the origin of internet

D) To attribute the origin of internet to telecommunications

Question 8

The following text is adapted from Edgar Rice Burroughs' 1912 novel *A Princess of Mars*. John Carter, the protagonist, is narrating his thoughts.

I have never told this story, nor shall mortal man see this manuscript until after I have passed over for eternity. I know that the average human mind will not believe what it cannot grasp. And so, I do not propose being pilloried by the public, and held up as a colossal liar when I am but telling the simple truths which some day science will substantiate. Possibly the suggestions which I gained from Mars, and the knowledge which can set down in this chronicle, will aid in an earlier understanding of our sister planet; <u>mysteries to you, but no longer mysteries to me</u>.

Which choice best describes the function of the underlined part in the text as a whole?

A) It gives the rationale behind the claim made in the second sentence.
B) It gives an exception for the author's claim in the earlier sentence.
C) It justifies the author's hope that is suggested in the earlier sentence.
D) It gives the reason for the author's statement in the first sentence.

Question 9

In Greek mythology, Pygmalion is a sculptor who loved his beautiful statue which he sculpted so much that it came to life. In an experiment popularly known as Pygmalion effect, psychologists Rosenthal and Jacobson informed faculty members of Oak Elementary School that some students, whose identifies were given to the teacher, had great academic potential. Unbeknown to the teachers, they were just randomly selected students. <u>This resulted in a self-fulfilling prophesy where the teachers unconsciously focused their energies on the 'high-performing' students</u>. These students were retested eight months later, and they did score significantly higher in the test.

Which choice best states the function of the underlined sentence in the overall structure of the text?

A) To draw a parallel between the teachers and the statue
B) To present a specific reason for the Pygmalion effect
C) To explain the importance of selection of students

D) To hint at the idea that the selected students did have great academic potential

Question 10

The following text is from *Songs of Travel and Other Verses,* a 1908 poetry anthology written by Robert Louis Stevenson.

> Or let autumn fall on me
> Where I afield I linger,
> Silencing the bird on tree,
> Biting the blue finger;
> White as meal the frosty field -
> Warm the fireside haven -
> Not to autumn will I yield,
> Not to winter even!

Which choice best states the main purpose of the text?

A) To describe the woes caused to a traveler by the inclement weather

B) To call attention to the poet's persistence in the face of unforgiving seasons

C) To reminisce about the difficulties faced by a traveler

D) To depict the poet's indifference to difficulties due to his love for travel

Question 11

The following text is adapted from A Comedy of Masks, a novel by Ernest Dowson and Arthur Moore published in 1893. Rainham, a dock proprietor, was talking to an artist who uses the property for his painting work.

> He looked up with a smile, in which an onlooker might have detected a spark of malice. He was a slight man of middle height, and of no apparent distinction, and his face with all its petulant lines of lassitude and ill-health – the wear and tear of forty years having done with him the work of fifty – struck one who saw Philip Rainham for the first time by nothing so much as by his ugliness. And yet few persons who knew him would have hesitated to allow to his nervous, suffering visage a certain indefinable charm.

According to the text, what is true about Rainham?

    A) He was almost always malicious.
    B) He was distinct from others in strange ways.
    C) He appeared older than he was.
    D) His sickly face looked grotesque to others.

Question 12

"The Garden" is a 1913 poem written by Ezra Pound. In the poem, Pound describes the internal conflict felt by a rich woman, who happens to watch poor kids in a garden.

Which quotation from "The Garden" most effectively describes the conflict?

    A) "And round about there is a rabble/ of filthy, sturdy, unkill-able infants of the very poor. / They shall inherit the earth."

B) "In her is the end of breeding. / Her boredom is exquisite and excessive."

C) "She would like someone to speak to her, / and is almost afraid that I / will commit that indiscretion."

D) "Like a skien of loose silk blown against a wall / She walks by the railing of a path in Kensington Gardens, / and she is dying piece-meal / of a sort of emotional anaemia."

Question 13

One of the founding fathers of Cubism, Albert Gleizes was in equal parts artist, theoretician, and philosopher and was responsible for bringing Cubism to the attention of the general public. However, some critics argue that Gleizes' art work took notable turn when, after his discharge from the army in 1915, he moved to New York where his work took on the frantic inspirations of life in that city.

Which of the following Gleizes' paintings would most directly support the critics' claim?

A) *Banks of the Marne* depicts a bright crimson sky that is pock-marked with purples and blues, making it a vigorous expression of the artist's subjectivity.

B) *Countryside* is a painting with his brushwork and also his choice of a single-perspective viewpoint reminisces some aspects of Impressionism.

C) *Woman with Phlox* stands as a revolutionary piece because it presents flattened forms and compressed space, depicting a seated woman staring down intently reading.

D) *Composition for "Jazz"* presents rudimentary elements of two performers both of whom are adorned in extravagant head-dress, a common attire of urban jazz players.

Question 14

Extinction rates during different geological periods of the Earth.

Name of the geological	Date	Intensity of extinction
Ordovician	- Ended 443 MYA	- 57% of genera lost - 86% of species lost
Late Devonian	- Ended 359 MYA	- 35% of genera lost. - 75% of species lost
Permian-Triassic	- Ended 251 MYA	- 56% genera lost - 96% of species lost
Triassic-Jurassic	- Ended 200 MYA	- 47% of genera lost - 80% of species lost

*MYA – Million Years Ago

Some researchers studying the major extinction episodes that happened on Earth have paid attention to the first four extinction episodes out of all the five major extinction episodes earth has faced; Ordovician, Late Devonian, Permian-Triassic, and Triassic-Jurassic periods. In fact, extinction figures given are merely estimates that have been arrived at by using fossil records. Basing on the information, they can conclusively conclude that _____.

Which choice most effectively uses data from the table to complete the argument?

A) Ordovician extinction resulted in loss of higher number of species than did Permian-Triassic extinction
B) highest number of species were lost during Permian-Triassic extinction
C) lowest proportion of genera were lost during Triassic-Jurassic extinction
D) after the four extinctions, most of the species were lost

Question 15

Species	hybrid zone		non-hybrid zone	
	Intra-specific reproduction	Inter-specific reproduction	Intra-specific reproduction	Inter-specific reproduction
Sphyrapicus ruber	72%	28%	89%	11%
Sphyrapicus nuchalis	86%	14%	94%	6%

James Smith and Patricia Anderson recently studied the frequency of inter-specific and intra-specific reproductions in two species of sapsuckers: red-breasted sapsucker (*Sphyrapicus ruber*) and red-naped sapsucker (*Sphyrapicus nuchalis*). Both these species of sapsuckers show more frequent inter-specific reproduction than all other species of sapsuckers. It is a proven fact that the chance of inter-specific reproduction is more in a hybrid zone than in a non-hybrid zone. The biologists also studied genetic diversity of both species in both the zones. Basing on their study, they concluded that genetic diversity is more pronounced in cases of reproduction when it happens inter-specifically than when it happens intra-specifically.

Which choice states an observation that, in combination with data from the table, best supports the researchers' conclusion?

A) The genetic diversity of both species is higher in hybrid zone than that in non-hybrid zone.
B) The genetic diversity of *S. nuchalis* in hybrid zone is more than that of *S. ruber* in hybrid zone.
C) The genetic diversity of *S. ruber* in non-hybrid zone is more than that of *S. ruber* in hybrid zone.
D) The genetic diversity of *S. nuchalis* in hybrid zone is less that in non-hybrid zone.

Prorocentrum cf. *balticum* is a microbe which can eat other microbes and can also prepare its food in photosynthesis. Biologists Michaela Larsson and Martina Doblin, who recently discovered this microbe, observed that this microbe can create a carbon sink that naturally removes carbon, which is the major reason for global warming. Having capacity to acquire nutrients in different ways means that this microbe can occupy parts of the ocean devoid of dissolved nutrients and therefore unsuitable for most phytoplankton. The biologists hypothesize that the existence of this microbe in such ocean parts will help oceans act as better natural carbon sink, when the effects of global warming become more pronounced in the future.

Which finding, if true, would most directly support the biologists' hypothesis?

A) *Prorocentrum* cf. *balticum* voraciously feeds on other phytoplankton that are currently present in ocean parts devoid of dissolved nutrients.

B) *Prorocentrum* cf. *balticum* can sequester carbon, even as oceans become more acidic due to global warming.

C) Currently, *Prorocentrum* cf. *balticum* contributes only to a tiny portion of carbon sequestration happening in ocean due to other phytoplankton.

D) Other species of phytoplankton act as carbon sinks because they remove carbon from circulation due to their metabolic processes.

Question 17

Worldwide environmental change resulting from the impact of a large celestial object with earth and/or from vast volcanic eruptions is commonly believed to be the reason for the extinction of dinosaurs at the boundary between Cretaceous and Paleogene eras, about 66 million years ago. However, there exists certain geological and paleontological evidence, such as the fossils showing their decline even during the Mesozoic era (252 million to 66 million years ago), the geological proof that different dinosaur species evolved rapidly and were quickly replaced by others throughout the Mesozoic and evidence that extant birds are theropod dinosaurs' lineage, proving that _____.

Which choice most logically completes the text?

A) the catastrophic event commonly believed to be the cause for the extinction was not the reason for the extinction of any dinosaur species

B) many factors other than the catastrophic event were responsible for the sudden disappearance of dinosaur species

C) many species other than dinosaurs became extinct in the aftermath of the catastrophic event

D) neither the purported extinction event was complete nor the catastrophic event was the sole cause for it

Question 18

A social construct is a concept that exists not in objective reality, but as a result of human interaction. It exists because humans agree that it exists. The concept that one person can 'murder' another person or one 'infringes on' the right of the other is a social construct, while 'killing' or 'snatching' an article from the other is a reality independent of human interaction or mutual human agreement. In legal proceedings, therefore, _____.

Which choice most logically completes the text?

A) judiciary seeks to judge the conflicting sides basing on the existence of the social construct, rather than on the legal merit

B) existence of social construct is an essentiality rather than a supplement, for law itself is a social construct

C) judgments are construed as valid and fair decisions depending only on the legal validity of the arguments presented by both sides

D) objective reality becomes the basis for offering judgments, regardless of subjective interpretations

Question 19

Designing effective conservation strategies must consider the location-specific needs of people who depend on forests for their livelihood. However, policy makers usually find _____ to be quite a challenging process, primarily because accurate information about the efficacy of strategies implemented in the past is rarely available.

Which choice completes the text so that it conforms to the conventions of Standard English?

A) them
B) theirs
C) its
D) it

Question 20

Traditionally, most boomerangs used by Aboriginal groups in Australia were non-returning. These weapons, sometimes called kylies, were used for hunting a variety of prey, from kangaroos to parrots; at a range of about 100 meters, a 2-kg non-returning boomerang could inflict mortal injury to a large animal.

  A) parrots; at
  B) parrots, at
  C) parrots. at
  D) parrots at

Question 21

In 1894, Maris Sklodowska (or Madam Curie, as she would be known as later) visited her family in Poland and was still labouring under the illusion that she would be able to work in her chosen field in Poland. However, she was denied a place by the male professors at Krakow University, though her qualifications were no less than _____, primarily because of sexism in academia.

Which choice completes the text so that it conforms to the conventions of Standard English?

  A) them
  B) they're
  C) their
  D) theirs

Question 22

Specifically referencing modern social media sites such as Facebook and Twitter, Eden Litt and Eszter Hargittai explain that the term *imagined audience* refers to a mental construct people form of their _____ who is actually consuming their online content.

Which choice completes the text so that it conforms to the conventions of Standard English?

A) audience, without real insight into,
B) audience without real insight into
C) audience; without real insight into
D) audience, without insight into

Question 23

The Great Depression (1929-1939) was an economic shock that impacted most countries across the world, resulting in economic disasters in almost all the countries in the world and Germany, which was already suffering in the aftermath of World War I, was no exception. The financial crisis there escalated out of control in mid-1931, _____ with the collapse of the Credit Anstalt, a major German bank, in Vienna in May.

Which choice completes the text so that it conforms to the conventions of Standard English?

A) started
B) being started
C) starting
D) to start

Migratory birds inherit from their parents the directions in which they need to migrate in the autumn and spring. If the parents each have a different genetically encoded directions, their offspring will end up with an intermediate _____ if a southwest-migrating bird is crossed with a southeast-migrating bird, their offspring will head south when the time comes.

Which choice completes the text so that it conforms to the conventions of Standard English?

    A) direction,
    B) direction:
    C) direction.
    D) direction

Question 25

Deep-sea fish live in regions where there is no natural illumination. Many of these are blind and rely on other senses, such as sensitivities to changes in local pressure and smell, to catch food and protect _____ from predators.

Which choice completes the text so that it conforms to the conventions of Standard English?

    A) itself
    B) it
    C) themselves
    D) them

Question 26

Endeavors with political and social ramifications beyond the playing field, many Native American games are seldom activities of frivolity and leisure. They can provide opportunities for expressions of cultural values and _____ other traditional activities, and thus, they can radiate potent symbolic meanings for participants and observers.

Which choice completes the text so that it conforms to the conventions of Standard English?

A) incorporating
B) incorporates
C) may incorporate
D) to incorporate

Question 27

In the past two decades, our understanding of the physiological feats that enable migratory birds to cross immense oceans, fly above the highest mountains, or remain in unbroken flight for months at a stretch, has _____ birds continually exceed what we think are the limits of physical endurance, like a six-inch sandpiper weighing less than an ounce flying 3,300 miles nonstop for six days from Canadian subarctic to South America.

Which choice completes the text so that it conforms to the conventions of Standard English?

A) been exploded, migrant
B) exploded. Migrant
C) exploded; migrant
D) exploded: migrant

Question 28

The American Civil War was among the first wars to utilize industrial warfare. Railroads, the telegraph, steamships, the ironclad warship, and mass-produced weapons were all widely used during the War. Resulting in around 700,000 deaths in soldiers, along with an undetermined number of civilian casualties, _____ making it the deadliest military conflict in American history.

Which choice completes the text so that it conforms to the conventions of Standard English?

    A) the Civil War resulted in carnage,
    B) the carnage of the Civil War resulted,
    C) the Civil War's carnage was resulted,
    D) it was the Civil War whose carnage was resulted,

Question 29

While there has been a lot of research on solar and nuclear energy as Martian energy sources, nuclear power harbours potential human risks and current models of solar systems lack the energy storage capability to compensate for day/night and seasonal variations in generation. It is, _____, prudent to consider an alternative source such as wind for stable power generation.

Which choice completes the text with the most logical transition?

    A) above all,
    B) on the other hand
    C) consequently,
    D) for instance

Question 30

Domesticating animals was difficult work for the ancient man. The easiest animals to domesticate were herbivores that graze on vegetation, because they were easiest to feed: they did not need humans to kill other animals to feed them, or to grow special crops. Cows, _____ were easily domesticated. Herbivores that eat grains were more difficult to domesticate than herbivores that graze because grains were valuable and also needed to be domesticated.

Which choice completes the text with the most logical transition?

A) similarly,
B) for instance,
C) coincidentally,
D) furthermore,

Question 31

In Europe, alchemy led to the discovery of manufacture of amalgams and advances in many other chemical processes. _____ by the 16th century, the alchemists in Europe had separated into two groups. The first focussed on the discovery of new compounds, leading to what is now Chemistry. The second continued to look at the more spiritual, metaphysical side of alchemy, continuing the search for immortality and the transmutation of base metals into gold.

Which choice completes the text with the most logical transition?

A) Ironically,
B) Eventually,
C) Surprisingly,
D) Additionally,

While researching a topic, a student has taken the following notes:

- Chronic mountain sickness (CMS) typically develops after extended time living at high altitude of over 3,000 metres (9,800 ft).
- In 1925, CMS was first discovered by Carlos Monge Medrano, who specialised in diseases of high altitude.
- While 28% people residing permanently at high altitudes develop CMS, around 14% of visitors to these areas develop this condition after two years of high-altitude life.
- Recent genetic research shows that 98% of people who become victims of CMS show ANP32D gene.
- Basing on these observations, scientists have concluded that a particular gene makes people more vulnerable.

The student wants to present the research and its findings. Which choice most effectively uses relevant information from the notes to accomplish this goal?

A) The focus of the recent genetic research was on the medical condition CMS, which was originally described by Carlos Monge Medrano way back in 1925.

B) The genetic research has identified a particular gene that is the primary cause for CMS, which is commonly found in people residing at high altitude regions.

C) While CMS, a medical condition first described by Carlos Monge Medrano, may be caused by high-altitude life, recent research has showed that a specific gene increases people's susceptibility to it.

D) Recent research has identified that a particular genetic abnormality is the reason for CMS, which is caused primarily in people living at high altitudes.

Question 33

While researching a topic, a student has taken the following notes:

- Slave narratives, the narratives of ex-slaves, were personal accounts of what it was like to live in slavery.
- They also provided Northerners and the world a glimpse into the life of slave communities.
- They provide the most powerful voices contradicting the slaveholders' favourable claims concerning slavery, becoming the abolitionist movement's voice of reality.
- On the other hand, Harlem Renaissance, a cultural movement taking place from 1919 into 1930s, represented and gave voice to the African American thought.
- Unlike the stereotypes of description of suffering in Slave Narratives, Harlem Renaissance celebrated black identity, depicting their racial pride.
- It paved the way for the civil rights movement.

The student wants to comment on the objectives of slave narratives and Harlem Renaissance literature in relation to African Americans. Which choice most effectively uses relevant information from the notes to accomplish this goal?

A) The former depicted physical suffering caused by slavery before emancipation and the latter depicted intellectual trauma caused by racial discrimination after abolition.
B) The former paved the way for emancipation by enlightening the world about suffering, and the latter paved the way for spiritual emancipation, and the quest for equality of rights as well.
C) The former led to constitutional remedy to the evil of slavery, and the latter depicted the intellectual turmoil in the aftermath of the evil of slavery.
D) The former paved the way for political rights, while the latter paved the way for civil rights.

22

A small request from the authors

If you find this book useful, your feedback encourages us and so don't forget to give feedback on Amazon.com or whatever website you have downloaded this book from.

If you want regular practice with new questions, consider visiting our website www.RRDigitalSAT.com, and register. You will enjoy the consistent journey by learning through our **SAT Question of the Day.**

READING AND WRITING MODULE 2

33 Questions

Directions: The questions in this section address a number of important reading and writing skills. Each question includes one or more passages, which may include a table or graph. Read each passage and question carefully, and then choose the best answer to the question based on the passage(s). All questions in this section are multiple-choice with four answer choices. Each question has a single best answer.

Question 1

The genesis of the American Civil War is obvious. Under Abraham Lincoln's leadership, the war was fought to preserve the Union. With slavery so deeply _____, Union leaders by 1862 had reached the decision that slavery had to end in order for the Union to be restored. Union war evolved as the war progressed in response to political and military issues.

Which choice completes the text with the most logical and precise word or phrase?

A) emotional
B) entrenched
C) divisive
D) involved

Question 2

Evolution is the cumulative effect of adaptations, but which adaptation gains ascendency over which is a point of interest. Predator-prey dynamics is certainly an important aspect. The relation between predator and prey is a bit like an evolutionary arms race. As soon as one develops a weapon or a defence mechanism, the other is working on an adaptation that allows it to _____ that mechanism.

Which choice completes the text with the most logical and precise word or phrase?

A) augment
B) assist
C) adapt
D) circumvent

Question 3

One human and animal behavior that has been observed for years, but is poorly understood, is yawning, which is clearly associated with sleepiness and boredom. However, almost _____, it is theorized that yawning is perhaps a reflex that your brain induces to wake you up or make you more alert. It has been observed that yawning is associated with release of some hormones that prune us for action.

Which choice completes the text with the most logical and precise word or phrase?

A) certainly
B) paradoxically
C) consciously
D) ridiculously

Question 4

Marquis de Condorcet, a radical thinker for his time and lineage, argued in 1780 that the rights of men stem exclusively from the fact that they are sentient beings, capable of acquiring moral ideas and of reasoning upon them. Since women have the same qualities, he argued, they _____ also have the same rights; either no member of the human race has any true rights, or else they all have the same ones.

Which choice completes the text with the most logical and precise word or phrase?

A) arguably
B) necessarily
C) prominently
D) tentatively

Question 5

Tamburlaine the Great is a play in two parts by Christopher Marlowe, and is loosely based on the life of the Central Asian emperor Timur. Written in 1587 or 1588, the play is _____ in Elizabethan public drama; it marks a turning away from the clumsy language and loose plotting of the earlier Tudor dramatists, and also marks a new interest in fresh and vivid language, memorable action and intellectual complexity.

Which choice completes the text with the most logical and precise word or phrase?

A) a benchmark
B) an achievement
C) a milestone
D) an exception

Question 6

In his book *The Fourth Amendment: Original Understanding and Modern Policing,* Michael J.Z. Mannheimer gives some observations. Police are required to obey the law. While that seems obvious, courts have lost track of that requirement due to _____ the constitutional provisions: the Fourth and the Fourteenth Amendments, which govern police conduct.

Which choice completes the text with the most logical and precise word or phrase?

A) overlapping
B) upholding
C) resorting to
D) misinterpreting

Question 7

In a meeting with legislators in September 1862, Otto Von Bismarck, Iron Chancellor who unified Germany, made a statement which would become _____: "The great questions of the day will not be decided by speeches and resolutions of majorities...but by blood and Iron." He later complained that his words were taken out of context and miscon-strued, but 'blood and iron' became a popular nickname for his policies.

Which choice completes the text with the most logical and precise word or phrase?

A) influential
B) notorious
C) proverbial
D) satirical

Question 8

The following text is from E. M. Forster's 1908 novel *A Room With A View*. Lucy Honeychurch, a Briton, was on tour to Italy and was in a hotel room.

It so happened that Lucy [Honeychurch], who found daily life rather chaotic, entered a more solid world when she opened the piano. She was then no longer either deferential or patronizing; no longer either a rebel or a slave. The kingdom of music is not the kingdom of this world; it will accept those whom breeding and intellect and culture have alike rejected. The commonplace person begins to play, and shoots into the empyrean without effort, whilst we look up, marvel-ling how he has escaped us, and thinking how we could worship him and love him.

Which choice best states the main purpose of the text?

A) To describe the feeling of divinity brought upon by appreciation of great music

B) To depict the ethereal nature of the composition on the piano

C) To describe how passionate Lucy was about music, which is beyond human bias

D) To bring out how Lucy compares to another person with great musical skills

Question 9

Text 1

Many drugs tested as effective cancer treatment failed in one crucial aspect: they also damage healthy tissues, causing serious side effects. Recently researchers modified a once-promising chemotherapy that had been abandoned due to damage it causes in gut tissues into a compound with "on" and "off" switches. The "on" switch was designed to be triggered by enzymes found in tumors, but not normal tissues, covering the compound into an active cancer drug. The 'off' switch, of course, is the enzyme produced by normal tissues.

Text 2

Dr Barbara Slusher who led a study of a new drug DRP-104 on mice said that the drug is as good at eliminating tumour as the original drug. In addition to directly killing tumor cells, the new drug also had another, equally important, effect in human clinical trials: it boosted the ability of a type of immune cell to kill cancer cells, helping to prevent tumors from coming back. "To have a drug that [not only] kills cancer cells but [also] activates immune cells is unique," Dr Slusher commented.

Based on the text, what would the author of Text 1 most likely to say about the study results mentioned in Text 2?

A) Though the new drug supports the optimization the modification presents, it presents a limitation needing our attention.
B) The study results have brought out a new benefit of our current research, despite the fact that they argue against our primary observation.
C) Besides endorsing our current research results, the results offer an added bonus to our expected result.
D) The results of our research are at variance with the results of that study, though their objective is common.

Question 10

The following text is adapted from William Shakespeare's 1609 poem "Sonnet 30". The poem describes the poet who is in pensive mood.

When to the sessions of sweet silent thought
I summon up remembrance of things past,
I sigh the lack of many a thing I sought,
And with old woes new wail my dear time's waste
Then can I drown an eye, unused to flow,
For precious friends hid in death's dateless night'
And weep afresh love's long since cancelled woe,
And moan the expense of many a vanished sight:

What is the main idea of the text?

A) The poet reminisces about the past and wastes his present which is valuable.
B) The poet remembers the past sorrows and compares them with the present's.
C) The poet remembers the sorrowful past and feels sad for wasting that time.
D) The poet remembers the regrets of the past and feels pensive again.

Question 11

The following text is adapted from Herman Melville's 1851 novel *Moby-Dick*. The following is the first-person narration of Ishmael, a character seeking employment as a sailor on a whaling boat.

What of it, if some old hunks of a sea-captain order me get a broom and sweep down the decks? What does that indignity amount to, weighed, I mean, in the scales of the New Testament? Do you think archangel Gabriel thinks anything the less of me, because I promptly and respectfully obey that old hunks in that particular instance?

Who ain't a slave? Tell me that.

Well, then, however the old sea-captains may order me about, I have the satisfaction of knowing that it is all right; that everybody else is one way or other served in much the same way; and so the universal thump is passed round, and all hands should rub each other's shoulder-blades, and be content.

Based on the text, how does Ishmael mentally respond to the treatment he might receive in the potential employment?

A) He fights back the temptation to undertake the employment, given the possibility of ill-treatment.
B) He entertains a resigned attitude given the inevitability of ill-treatment in most walks of life.
C) He considers himself lucky to find employment as a sailor, despite the ill-treatment that is in store for him.
D) He becomes resigned towards the ill-treatment because of his deep religious beliefs he entertains.

The adventures of Ferdinand, Count Fathom is a 1753 novel by Tobias Smollett. Sir Walter Scott commented that the novel paints a "complete picture of human depravity (moral corruption)": _____

Which quotation (adapted for access to modern readers) from the book most effectively illustrates Scott's comment?

A) "Having thus inflamed her (Teresa's) love of pleasure, he hinted his design upon the young lady's (Teresa's employer's) fortune and promised Teresa that could he once make himself legal possessor of Mademoiselle, his dear Teresa should reap the happy fruits of his affluence."

B) "It was impossible for her (Teresa's employer) to overlook such studied emotions; she in a jocose manner taxed him with having lost his heart, rallied the excess of his passion, and in a merry strain undertook to be an advocate for his love."

C) "It would have been impossible for the mother of our adventurer, such as she hath been described, to sit quietly in her tent, which such an heroic scene was acting."

D) "Meanwhile, Ferdinand improved apace in the accomplishments of infancy; his beauty was conspicuous, and his vigour so uncommon, that he was with justice, likened unto Hercules in the cradle."

Question 13

Scores given for two different scorers basing on different parameters
and the correlation between the scores

Category	Scorer A (mean)	Scorer B (mean)	Correlation
Content	2.99	3.10	0.70
Organization	3.99	3.40	0.70
Coherence & cohesion	3.65	2.86	0.67
Vocabulary use	2.69	2.78	0.81
Grammar & usage	2.62	3.39	0.85

In research on evaluation, a set of analytical essays written in English were evaluated by two scorers: Scorer A (a Japanese scorer) and Scorer B (a native English-speaking scorer). The essays were given scores (on a range of 1 to 5) basing on five parameters: content, organization, coherence & cohesion, vocabulary use, grammar and usage. Basing on the observations, the researchers claim that the correlation between the two scorers is high when the parameter used is an objective one related to compliance to rules rather than a subjective one judging standards.

Which choice best describes data from the table that support the researcher' claim?

A) Scorer B gives a higher mean score than Scorer A when the parameter is Content.

B) The Organization mean score of Scorer A is higher than his Content mean score.

C) The correlations between Scorer A and Scorer B are the same for two different parameters: Content and Organization.

D) The correlation between Scorer A and Scorer B is higher in Grammar & usage than it is in Content.

Question 14

Christopher Hsee, a professor of Behavioral Science and Marketing, Booth School of Business argues that value perception is a fundamental aspect that makes marketing success, because value, a sense of worth, usefulness, or importance attached to something in this context, decides a purchase decision. People do not know what they want if you ask them. They decide what they want after reviewing context and comparative evaluation is easier. Psychologists have claimed to have found evidence for Christopher's claim in a recent study in which same volume of ice-cream of same quality was sold.

Which finding from the study, if true, would most strongly support Christopher's explanation for marketing success?

A) An ice cream vender selling ice cream at a larger shop sells as much ice cream as one selling at a smaller shop.

B) A vender selling the ice cream in smaller tubs sold more ice cream than the same ice cream in larger tubs.

C) A downtown ice cream vendor sells more ice cream than the one selling it in sub-urbs.

D) An ice cream brand that is more advertised during summer than it is during winter.

Question 15

The table below compares GDP per capita (in US dollars) indicating the economic growth, at the technological frontier, of four countries: The United States of America, the United Kingdom, Japan and China between 1960 and 2000.

Name of the country	1960	1970	1980	1990	2000
America	18,175	23,691	29,949	36,982	45,886
Britain	14,118	16,593	20,612	26,189	33,211
Japan	7,164	12,725	21,404	29,949	31,946
China	874	1,178	1,930	2,982	4,730

During the forty years under study, there was growth in per capita GDP (in US dollars) of the four countries which are compared. However, the per capita growth in GDP in countries near technological frontiers (America and Britain) is less pronounced than that in countries (Japan and China) that are far away from the technological frontier. This growth rate difference is most clearly seen by comparing _____

Which choice most effectively uses data from the table to complete the statement?

A) the growth in Japan between 1960 and 2000 and that in China between the same years.

B) the growth in China between 1960 and 2000 and that in America between the same years.

C) the growth in Britain between 1960 and 2000 and that in America between the same years.

D) the growth in America between 1990 and 2000 and that in Britain between the same years.

Question 16

A software company has recently claimed that it has created an AI-software that undertakes creating writing as effectively as a highly creative human can. To make the writing thus created by the software 'natural', the scientists created the database of ten thousand human-created samples of fiction, which the software uses to model its output after. While the supporters of the software argue that creating a best seller soon requires knowledge of just some computer commands to be used by the software, critics argue that the software will never be able to replace creative writers.

Which of the following, if true, would most directly support the critics' argument?

A) The development of the software has required a lot of resources, and consequently, the program is likely to be very costly to buy.

B) The software requires as input complex information that decides different parameters to be used in the production of a creative work.

C) Spontaneity in writing is required to decide the flow of plot and this feature cannot be programmed in a software.

D) Artificial intelligence, the basis for the software, is being used in many fields to minimize human error.

Question 17

More than 5,000 exoplanets have been discovered since the first one was discovered in 1995. To qualify as potentially life-friendly, a planet must be relatively small (and therefore rocky) and orbit in the 'habitable zone' of its star, which is loosely defined as a location where water can exist in liquid form on a world's surface. None of the exoplanets discovered till now hardly qualify for these conditions. However, this 'life-friendly' is just earth-like life-friendly, and these exoplanets thus

_____

Which choice most logically completes the text?

    A) may contain life in a form which is totally unfamiliar to us.
    B) might not contain earth-like life forms.
    C) are likely to be planets that are in habitable zones.
    D) are likely to contain earth-life at least with some probability.

Question 18

Severe mental disorders, which are common, differ from severe physical disorders caused by mutations in a single gene, which appear very infrequently. For instance, achondroplastic dwarfism, the result of single gene mutation, does not occur in more than 4 in 100,000 people. However, mental disorders such as bipolar disorder and mental retardation affects around 1000 in 100,000 people. The fertility estimates of people with mental disorders are lower than norm. if it is the case that these disorders harmed reproductive success over evolutionary time, then these variant form of genes that predispose people to mental disorders should have been wiped out many millennia ago. The prevalence of such mental disorders suggests that _____

Which choice most logically completes the text?

    A) in periods shorter than evolutionary time, severe mental disorders are contained effectively.

B) severe physical disorders due to genetic mutations are more detrimental to evolution than are severe mental disorders.

C) evolution sometimes presents results not expected, creating an evolutionary paradox.

D) severe mental disorders should have some beneficial effect on the evolutionary process.

Question 19

In Don Paterson's most recent collection, *The Arctic,* the poet is doing what he has always done best: these poems are formally adept, sharp, philosophical, funny. What is really exciting, however, is the that venturing into a new ground altogether – somewhere darker, less enlightened, harder to escape through verse – _____ this collection fresh and inviting.

Which choice completes the text so that it conforms to the conventions of Standard English?

A) make
B) are making
C) makes
D) have made

Question 20

The global prevalence of anxiety and depression soaring by as much as 25% during the first year of Covid19 pandemic, the lockdown splintered people's mental _____ sign of caution for healthcare providers and governments to track mental health issues with vigilance.

Which choice completes the text so that it conforms to the conventions of Standard English?

A) health, which is a
B) health. A
C) health; a
D) health, a

Question 21

In his book *The Journeys of Trees*, Zach St. George explores an agonizingly slow migration of forests. A forest sends seeds just beyond its footprint in every direction, but the seeds that go to the north – assuming the north is the more hospitable direction – thrive a little more than the ones that fall to the south, _____ in the long run a slow, but steady forest migration, which unfortunately cannot keep pace with climate change.

Which choice completes the text so that it conforms to the conventions of Standard English?

A) causes
B) to cause
C) caused
D) causing

The Bluest Eye (1970) is Toni Morrison's novel that depicts the story of Pecola Breedlove, a young African-American marginalized by her community and the larger society. A powerful interrogation of _____ to an idea of beauty, the book asks vital questions about race, class and gender and remains one of Morrison's most unforgettable works.

Which choice completes the text so that it conforms to the conventions of Standard English?

A) what does it mean to conform,
B) what it means to conform
C) what conformity means: as
D) what does it mean to conform?

Question 23

The physiological response to exercise is dependent on the intensity, duration and frequency of the exercise as well as on the environmental conditions. During physical exercise, requirements for oxygen and substrate in skeletal muscle are increased, just as _____ the removal of metabolites and carbon dioxide.

Which choice completes the text so that it conforms to the conventions of Standard English?

A) are
B) is
C) do
D) will be

Question 24

On October 29, 1969, the UCLA professor Leonard Kleinrock and his student Charley Kline electronically sent Stanford University researcher Bill Duval the first message "lo", because the complete intended message "login" could not be sent because of system crash after entering the letter _____ subsequent improvements, roughly 450.4 billion emails, which contain data equal to information in almost a trillion books, were sent and received each day in 2022.

Which choice completes the text so that it conforms to the conventions of Standard English?

A) "o", after
B) "o". After
C) "o"; after
D) "o": after

Question 25

Rates at which young forests remove carbon from the atmosphere vary by orders of magnitude across the world; tropical countries in Central Africa have the highest rates, while countries in Central Europe have the lowest. By harmonizing detailed carbon measurement collected at different locations and combining them with cutting edge machine learning tools, an advanced computer model can consider different variables and _____ a viable solution for environmental problems.

Which choice completes the text so that it conforms to the conventions of Standard English?

A) develop
B) develops
C) developing
D) developed

Question 26

Responsible for nearly 25 deaths per terawatt-hour of electricity produced, _____ the deadliest power source.

Which choice completes the text so that it conforms to the conventions of Standard English?

A) 35% of electricity worldwide is generated by coal,
B) the generation of 35% of world electricity is by coal, which is
C) world electricity's share of 35% is generated by coal,
D) coal, which generates 35% of electricity worldwide, is

Question 27

DNA of Neanderthals, human ancestors that became extinct millions of years ago, pose many technical challenges to develop their genome because with time DNA becomes chemically modified and after thousands of years it is massively contaminated with DNA from bacteria. In his seminal study, Swedish _____ made discoveries concerning genomes of extinct hominins, an endeavour lasting several decades and winning him Nobel Prize.

A) geneticist, Svante Pääbo,
B) geneticist Svante Pääbo,
C) geneticist Svante Pääbo
D) geneticist, Svante Pääbo

Question 28

An obvious difference between freshwater and seawater habitats is salt concentration. Freshwater fish maintain the physiological mechanisms that permit them to concentrate salts within their bodies in a salt-deficient environment; Marine fish, _____ excrete excess salts in an environment with high salt concentration.

Which choice completes the text with the most logical transition?

A) consequently
B) for example,
C) on the other hand,
D) by definition

Question 29

Structural color was documented in the 17th century, in peacock feathers, but it is only since the invention of the electron microscope, in 1930s, that we have known how it works. Structural color is completely different from pigment color. Pigments are molecules that absorb light, except for the wavelengths corresponding to the visible color. _____ intricate nanoscale architectures of structural color do not absorb light but reflect it into particular wavelengths resulting in vivid, often shimmering colors.

Which choice completes the text with the most logical transition?

A) Accordingly,
B) In contrast,
C) Presumably,
D) Similarly,

Question 30

Sonam Wangchuk, a technologist, innovator and social and climate change activist, has a deep understanding of his region. The entire Himalayan ecology is under pressure and the people of Ladakh have started experiencing the manifestations of climate change. In the scenario, Sonam has radically different views about the potential solutions. He, _____, needs to be heard, for he is informed, credible and sincere and is speaking on the basis of his experience.

Which choice completes the text with the most logical transition?

A) in other words,
B) surprisingly,
C) however,
D) to summarize

Question 31

While researching a topic, a student has taken the following notes:

- Gestation in mammals is the time between conception and birth, during which the fetus is developing in the womb.
- The length of gestation varies from species to species and also the breeding seasons of these species are restricted.
- The horse, a spring breeder with 11 months' gestation, has its young the following spring.
- The sheep, a fall breeder with a five months' gestation, has its young the following spring.
- During spring, food is most abundant for the grazing animals.

The student wants to correlate the gestation with the season in which the birth takes place. Which choice most effectively uses relevant information from the notes to accomplish this goal?

A) The length of gestation is independent of the season in which birth takes place.
B) Gestation is adjusted so that birth coincides with the period when food is most abundant.
C) Both the size of the breeding animal and length of gestation coincide with the season in which birth takes place.
D) Gestation period is a variant of the animal breeding during certain seasons only.

Question 32

While researching a topic, a student has taken the following notes:

- Recent research helped understand the relationship between blood pressure and blood viscosity (a factor showing 'thickness of blood').
- The study observed 49 normal subjects and 49 patients with untreated hypertension (high blood pressure).
- Systolic viscosity (viscosity when heart contracts) was 10% higher in hypertensive patients than in people with normal blood pressure.
- Diastolic blood viscosity (viscosity when heart dilates) was 25% higher in hypertensive patients than in people normal blood pressure.
- Systolic blood pressure is always higher than diastolic blood pressure in all subjects.

The student wants to provide an explanation for high blood pressure by connecting it to blood viscosity. Which choice most effectively uses relevant information from the notes to accomplish this goal?

A) The systolic and diastolic viscosities of blook are higher in hypertensive people than they are in people with normal blood pressure.

B) Normal people have higher systolic blood pressure than their diastolic blood pressure.

C) Systolic blood pressure in hypertensive people is higher than their diastolic blood pressure.

D) For some people, the viscosity of blood is higher than that in some other people.

Question 33

While researching a topic, a student has taken the following notes:

- Era of Good Feelings was said to reflect the national mood of the United States between 1815 and 1825.
- Although it is considered coexistent with James Monroe's two terms (1817-1825), it really began in 1815 during the last years of James Madison's presidency.
- The good feelings started with U. S's enactment of protective tariff and the establishment of the second National Bank.
- With sectional conflicts in abeyance, nationalism seemed to pervade the national mood.
- But by 1820, a longer conflict, especially due to slavery issue, was in in the offing, imperceptibly though.
- The era proved to be a temporary lull in conflict, while new issues were emerging.

The student wants to emphasize the misconception the name 'Era of Good Feelings' is likely to create. Which choice most effectively uses relevant information from the notes to accomplish this goal?

A) The Era of Good Feelings is wrongly said to coexist with Monroe's terms, while in fact it started earlier.

B) The sectional conflicts that were in abeyance were not an indication of nationalism during Era of Good Feelings.

C) The conflicts before the Era of Good Feelings were not as divisive as those after that Era.

D) The name Era of Good Feelings is a misnomer since it actually hid hostilities that would evolve into major conflicts.

A small request from the authors

If you find this book useful, your feedback encourages us and so don't forget to give feedback on Amazon.com or whatever website you have downloaded this book from.

If you want regular practice with new questions, consider visiting our website www.RRDigitalSAT.com, and register. You will enjoy the consistent journey by learning through our **SAT Question of the Day.**

MATH MODULE 1

27 questions

Directions

The questions in this section address a number of important math skills.

Use of a calculator is permitted for all questions.

Notes

Unless otherwise indicated:

- All variables and expressions represent real numbers.
- Figures provided are drawn to scale.
- All figures lie in a plane
- The domain of a given function f is the set of all real numbers x for which $f(x)$ is a real number.

Reference

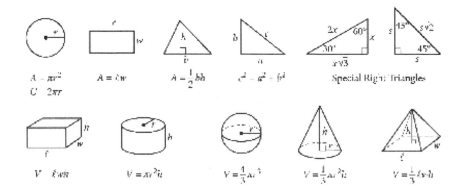

$A = \pi r^2$

$C = 2\pi r$

$A = \ell w$

$A = \frac{1}{2} bh$

$c^2 = a^2 + b^2$

Special Right Triangles

$V = \ell w h$

$V = \pi r^2 h$

$V = \frac{4}{3} \pi r^3$

$V = \frac{1}{3} \pi r^2 h$

$V = \frac{1}{3} \ell w h$

The number of degrees of arc in a circle is 360
The number of radians of arc in a circle is 2Π
the sum of the measures in degrees of the angles of a triangle is 180.

Question 1

What is 20% of 10% of 3500?

A) 70

B) 105

C) 630

D) 1050

Question 2

The price, p, in dollars, of an item is calculated by the equation $p = 2(1.1n + 10)$, where n represents the number of years since the item goes on sale. Which equation has the same solution as the given equation?

A) $p = 2.2n + 10$

B) $\frac{p}{2} = 1.1n + 20$

C) $p = 2.2n + 20$

D) $\frac{p}{2} = 2.2n + 20$

Question 3

In a certain class of n students, one-third of them use blue ink. Of these, one-fourth also use black ink. The number of students who use both blue ink and black ink is at least 3. Which inequality represents this situation?

A) $n \leq 36$

B) $n \geq 4$

C) $\dfrac{n^2}{12} \geq 3$

D) $n \geq 36$

Question 4

The functions f and g are defined by $f(x) = x + 1$ and $g(x) = 2x^2 - 1$. For what value of x is $f(g(x)) = 32$?

A) 2

B) 4

C) 7

D) 9

Question 5

$$p = n^2 - 1$$

If n is a number chosen at random from the set {2, 3, 5, 7, 11, 13, 15, 17, 19}, what is the probability that p is a prime?

A) $\frac{1}{9}$

B) $\frac{2}{9}$

C) $\frac{7}{9}$

D) $\frac{8}{9}$

Question 6

Machine A bakes bread twice as fast as machine B. Machine B bakes 25 loaves of bread in 10 minutes. If both machines bake bread at a constant rate, how many loaves of bread does machine A bake in 4 minutes?

Question 7

The function f is defined by the equation $f(x) = 3x - 8$. If $f(a + 3) = 10$, what is the value of a?

Question 8

During summer, the local amusement park sells tickets at discounted price for groups of students. For a group of n students, it sells tickets at d dollars for each ticket for the first 20 students, and offers a discount of p dollars for each ticket purchased after the first 20. Which equation represents the total cost of the tickets for n students, assuming $n > 20$?

A) $20d + (20 - n)(d - p)$

B) $20d + (n - 20)(d - p)$

C) $20d + p(n - 20)$

D) $20d + p(20 - n)$

Question 9

Triangles ABC and XYZ are similar, where A and B correspond to X and Y respectively. Angle Y has a measure of 90^0. $XY = 12$ centimeters, $YZ = 16$ centimeters and $AB = 20$ centimeters. What is the value of $\sin A$?

A) $\frac{3}{5}$

B) $\frac{2}{3}$

C) $\frac{4}{5}$

D) $\frac{4}{3}$

Question 10

$$x = 3k + y$$
$$y = x - 6$$

The system of equations is true for all values (x, y), and k is a constant. What is the value of k?

A) 0

B) 1

C) 2

D) 3

Question 11

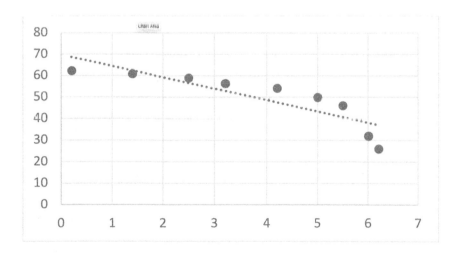

A line of best fit is shown for a given set of data points. Which of the following equations is the most appropriate linear model for the data points?

A) $y = -5.27x + 70$

B) $y = 5.27x + 70$

C) $y = -5.27x$

D) $y = -5.27x - 70$

Question 12

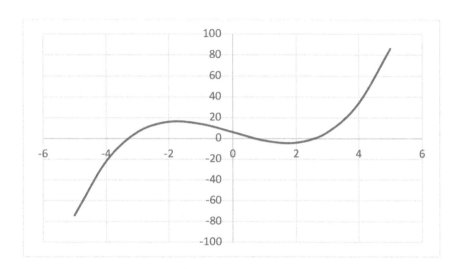

The graph of $y = f(x) = x^3 - 9x + 6$ is shown. For how many values of x does $f(x) = 0$?

A) Zero

B) One

C) Two

D) Three

Question 13

A math professor intends to convert a raw score x on a test into a new scaled score y by using a simple linear function $y = mx + c$.

According to this function, a student who gets a raw score of 90 receives a scaled score of 100. But, a student who gets a raw score of 65 receives a scaled score of 85. What is the value of m?

Question 14

x	2	3
y	-1	a

If the relation between x and y can be best represented by $y = x^2 - kx + 1$, what is the value of a?

Question 15

A group of students volunteered for a community cause. It was observed that for each hour that passed while completing a specific task, the time taken by each student to complete a similar task decreased by 10%. Phil took 2 hours to complete a task when he started initially. Which equation represents the amount of time H, in hours, that Phil will take to complete the task after n hours?

A) $H = 2(0.1)^n$

B) $H = n(0.1)^2$

C) $H = 2(0.9)^n$

D) $H = 2(0.1n)^2$

Question 16

Which expression is equivalent to $\frac{5x^2-13x-6}{x-3}$?

A) $5x - 2$

B) $x - 3$

C) $5(x - 3)$

D) $5x + 2$

Question 17

The cost of manufacturing a refrigerator consists of the average cost of plastic materials, p, and the average cost of electronics, e. The total cost of manufacturing a refrigerator is t, and the situation is represented by the equation $pn + em = t$. Which of the following is the best interpretation of m in this context?

A) The average number of plastic materials used for a refrigerator in the manufacturing

B) The average number of electronics used for a refrigerator in the manufacturing

C) The total number of plastic materials used in the manufacturing

D) The total number of electronics used in the manufacturing

No. of Units Leased	Rental Value (dollars)
75	800
70	1000
65	1200
60	1400
55	1600
50	1800
45	2000

The table shows the relationship between the rental values, y, of different condominiums and the number of units leased, x. Which equation most accurately represents this relationship?

A) $y = -40x + 3800$

B) $40x + y = -3800$

C) $y = 40x + 3800$

D) $40y = -x + 3800$

Question 19

The circumference of circle C is 18π. The radius of circle D is $2k$, where k is the diameter of circle C. The area of circle D is how many times greater than the area of circle C?

A) 9

B) 15

C) 16

D) 1226

Question 20

Data Value (degrees Fahrenheit)	Frequency
85	4
88	7
90	3
94	6
97	7
101	2
104	2

The frequency table gives information about temperatures, in degrees Fahrenheit, recorded in a city during a 31-day period. What is the median temperature, in degrees Fahrenheit, of the data set?

Question 21

A circle in the xy-plane passes through the point (3, 1). The equation of the circle is $x^2 + y^2 - 6x + 8y - c = 0$, where c is a constant. What is the radius of the circle?

Question 22

The angle made by arc AB at the center of a circle is $\frac{3\pi}{4}$ radians. Arc BC makes an angle $\frac{7\pi}{12}$ radians at the center of the circle. What is the measure of the angle, in <u>degrees</u>, made by arc CA at the center of the circle?

A) 105

B) 120

C) 250

D) 270

Question 23

The age of the Sun is approximately 4.603×10^9 years, and one year is approximately 3.2×10^7 seconds. Which of the following is closest to the age of the Sun, in seconds?

A) 7.80×10^{16}

B) 12×10^{16}

C) 1.47×10^{17}

D) 14.73×10^{63}

Question 24

The graph of line m is the result of shifting the graph of line l 4 units right and 2 units up in the xy-plane. Line l is represented by the equation $3x - 2y + 6 = 0$. What is the y-intercept of line m?

A) (0, -4)

B) (0, -2)

C) (0, -1)

D) (0, 1)

Question 25

In the xy-plane, the graph of $x^2 + y^2 = 16$ intersects $y = x^2 + 2$ at how many points of intersection?

A) 0

B) 1

C) 2

D) 4

Question 26

$$5x - 3y = 10$$
$$ax + by = 4$$

In the xy-plane, the graphs of the two equations intersect at 90 degrees at (5, 5). What is the value of b?

A) $\frac{3}{10}$

B) $\frac{1}{2}$

C) 3

D) 5

Question 27

The sides of a triangle are 9 centimeters, 12 centimeters and p centimeters. For what value of p, in centimeters, will the triangle have the greatest area, in square centimeters?

A small request from the authors

If you find this book useful, your feedback encourages us and so don't forget to give feedback on Amazon.com or whatever website you have downloaded this book from.

If you want regular practice with new questions, consider visiting our website www.RRDigitalSAT.com, and register. You will enjoy the consistent journey by learning through our **SAT Question of the Day.**

MATH MODULE 2

27 questions

Directions

The questions in this section address a number of important math skills.

Use of a calculator is permitted for all questions.

Notes

Unless otherwise indicated:

- All variables and expressions represent real numbers.
- Figures provided are drawn to scale.
- All figures lie in a plane
- The domain of a given function f is the set of all real numbers x for which $f(x)$ is a real number.

Reference

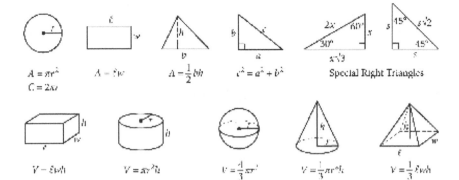

$A = \pi r^2$
$C = 2\pi r$

$A = \ell w$

$A = \frac{1}{2} bh$

$c^2 = a^2 + b^2$

Special Right Triangles

$V = \ell w h$

$V = \pi r^2 h$

$V = \frac{4}{3} \pi r^3$

$V = \frac{1}{3} \pi r^2 h$

$V = \frac{1}{3} \ell w h$

The number of degrees of arc in a circle is 360
The number of radians of arc in a circle is 2Π
the sum of the measures in degrees of the angles of a triangle is 180.

66

Question 1

A laser printer prints y pages in t minutes. Which expression represents the amount of time, in hours, the printer takes to print $100y$ pages?

A) $\frac{t}{60}$

B) $\frac{t}{100}$

C) $\frac{3t}{5}$

D) $\frac{5t}{3}$

Question 2

Betty drives t hours at a constant speed of 60 miles per hour to cover a distance of s miles. Which equation models the distance s if she increases her speed by k miles per hour so she can cover the distance in n fewer hours?

A) $s = (60 + k)(t - n)$

B) $s = \frac{60+t}{t-n}$

C) $s = k(t - n) - 60$

D) $s = 60k\left(\frac{t}{n}\right)$

Question 3

$$5x + y = 5$$
$$-cx + 2y = 10$$

In the system of equations, c is a constant and the given system of equations has a unique solution (x, y). Which of the following is true of c ?

A) $c = -10$

B) $c = 10$

C) $c \neq -10$

D) $c > 10$

Question 4

A taxi cab covers a distance of s miles in t hours arriving 40 minutes earlier than the scheduled time. What should the speed of the cab, in miles per hour, be if it were to arrive on time?

A) $\dfrac{s}{t+40}$

B) $\dfrac{3s}{3t-2}$

C) $\dfrac{s}{3t-2}$

D) $\dfrac{3s}{3t+2}$

Question 5

The angles of a triangle are in the ratio 1:1:2 and the length of one of the shorter sides is 5 units. What is the length of the longest side of the triangle?

A) $2\sqrt{5}$

B) $5\sqrt{2}$

C) 10

D) $10\sqrt{2}$

Question 6

Three times the first of 3 consecutive even integers, when placed in an increasing order, is 2 more than twice the third. What is the second even integer?

A) 10

B) 12

C) 14

D) 16

Question 7

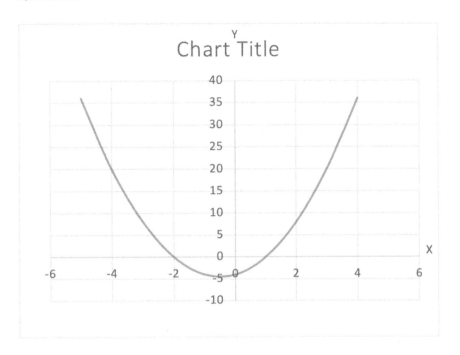

The y-intercept of the graph $y = 2x^2 + 2x - 4$ is $(0, y)$. What is the value of y?

Question 8

The function g is defined by $g(x) = 3x - 7$. What is the x-intercept of the graph of $y = g(-x)$ in the xy-plane?

A) -7

B) $-\dfrac{7}{3}$

C) $-\dfrac{3}{7}$

D) $\dfrac{7}{3}$

Question 9

The function h is defined by $h(x) = |x - 2|$. Which of the following represents $i(x)$, where $i(x)$ is the result of shifting the graph of $h(x)$ 3 units up and 4 units right?

A) $i(x) = |x - 6|$

B) $i(x) = |x - 6| + 3$

C) $i(x) = |x + 2| + 3$

D) $i(x) = |x - 6| - 3$

Question 10

$$16^x = 2$$
$$x^y = 64$$

Which ordered pair (x, y) is a solution to the given system of equations?

A) $\left(-\frac{1}{4}, -3\right)$

B) $\left(-\frac{1}{4}, 3\right)$

C) $\left(\frac{1}{4}, -3\right)$

D) $\left(\frac{1}{4}, 3\right)$

Question 11

Which expression is equivalent to $\dfrac{2x}{3x^2+6x} + \dfrac{x-1}{x+2}$, where $x \neq 0$?

A) $\dfrac{3x-1}{3(x+2)}$

B) $\dfrac{x-1}{x+2}$

C) $\dfrac{3x-1}{3x^2+7x+2}$

D) $\dfrac{6x-1}{3x^2+7x+2}$

Question 12

The function g is defined by $g(x) = 3x^2 - 5x + k$, where k is a constant. What is value of k when $g(1) = 0$?

A) -2

B) 0

C) 2

D) 1

Question 13

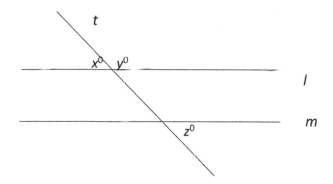

Note: Figure not drawn to scale.

In the figure shown, line t intersects parallel lines l and m. $x = 4p + 17$, $z = 9p - 13$, where p is a constant. What is the value of y ?

Question 14

In the list of data values

$$24, 18, 48, 30, x$$

the arithmetic mean, median and mode are all equal. What is the value of x ?

Question 15

The equation $C(n)=100(1.15)^n$ gives the estimated cost of production of manufacturing a total of k items, where n is the number of years since the item is in production. Which of the following is the best interpretation of the number 15 in this context?

A) The percent increase in the estimated cost of production each year for k items

B) The increase in the absolute value of the estimated cost of production for each of the k items

C) The initial value of the estimated cost of production per each item

D) The increase in production over k items each year

Question 16

$$f(x) = -2x^2 + 4x + 5$$

Which of the following is true of $f(x)$?

A) The minimum value of $f(x)$ is 5.

B) The minimum value of $f(x)$ is 7.

C) The maximum value of $f(x)$ is 5.

D) The maximum value of $f(x)$ is 7.

Question 17

Every fortnight, Marie sets aside $100 from her earnings towards her savings. Which of the following accurately describes how the value of her savings changes as a function of time?

A) Linear and decreases with time

B) Exponential and decreases with time

C) Linear and increases with time

D) Exponential and increases with time

Question 18

On a standardized test, 40% of the 400 students from Glendale High School scored 90th percentile while 40% of the 500 students from Rockwel High School scored 90th percentile. The total number of students who score 90th percentile from both the schools is times the total number of students from both the schools. What is the value of ?

A) $\frac{2}{5}$

B) $\frac{4}{9}$

C) $\frac{5}{2}$

D) 360

Which of the following is equivalent to $\dfrac{32 \times \sqrt[3]{81} \times \sqrt{125}}{30}$?

A) $2^4 \times \sqrt[3]{3}$

B) $2^4 \times \sqrt[3]{3} \times \sqrt{5}$

C) $2^5 \times \sqrt[3]{3} \times \sqrt{5}$

D) $2^4 \times 3\sqrt[3]{3} \times 5\sqrt{5}$

Question 20

A man purchases two different types of toys – the first type at \$9 each and the second at \$5 each. He spends a maximum of \$115. What is the ratio of the number of toys of the second type to the first type so that a maximum number of toys of the first type are purchased at no additional cost? *(Express ratio as a fraction)*

For $|3x - 5| = 16$, if $(7, 0)$ and $(x, 0)$ are the two x-intercepts, what is the value of x?

Explanation

Brain/Paper Work:

The absolute value equation can be written as two separate linear equations –

$3x - 5 = 16$ and $-(3x - 5) = 16$

From the first equation, $3x = 21$ or $x = 7$ (this value is already given).

From the second equation,

$-3x + 5 = 16$

$-3x = 11$

$x = -\dfrac{11}{3}$

Answer:

Thus, the correct answer is $-\dfrac{11}{3}$.

Question 22

A cylindrical pail has a radius of 7 inches and height of 9 inches. If there are 231 cubic inches to a gallon, approximately, how many gallons will this pail hold?

A) 2

B) 6

C) 231

D) 1386

Question 23

What is the circumference of the circle in the xy-plane with equation $x^2 + y^2 - 10x + 14y - 7 = 0$?

A) 9π

B) 14π

C) 18π

D) 81π

Question 24

n years after 2012, the population of city X is given by the function $f(x) = 25000(1.05)^n$, and that of city Y is given by the function $g(x) = 40000(0.97)^n$. Which of the following accurately describes the functions $f(x)$ and $g(x)$?

A) $f(x)$ is increasing linear and $g(x)$ is decreasing linear

B) $f(x)$ is increasing exponential and $g(x)$ is decreasing linear

C) $f(x)$ is decreasing exponential and $g(x)$ is increasing exponential

D) $f(x)$ is increasing exponential and $g(x)$ is decreasing exponential

Question 25

Steve lends $100 to Pat at 2 percent interest compounded annually, and uses the function $f(x) = 100(r)^n$ to calculate the total amount due to him after n years. Pat, in turn, lends the $100 to Kiran at 3 percent interest compounded annually, and uses the function $g(x) = 100(p)^n$ to calculate the total amount due to him after n years. Which of the following equations represents the relationship between r and p ?

A) $p = r + 0.01$

B) $p = r + 0.1$

C) $r = p - 1$

D) $r = p + 0.01$

Question 26

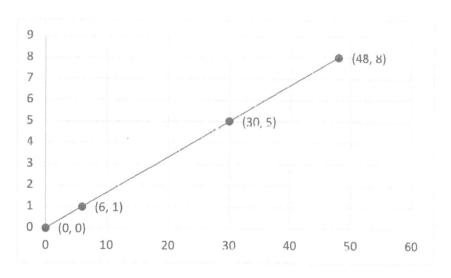

In the xy-plane, how many coordinate points with integer coordinates lie on the line joining $(0, 0)$ and $(48, 8)$, including the end-points $(0, 0)$ and $(48, 8)$?

A) 4

B) 7

C) 9

D) 49

Question 27

$$3x^2 - 5x + k = 0$$

In the given equation, k is an integer, and the equation has real solutions. What is the greatest possible value of k?

A small request from the authors

If you find this book useful, your feedback encourages us and so don't forget to give feedback on Amazon.com or whatever website you have downloaded this book from.

If you want regular practice with new questions, consider visiting our website www.RRDigitalSAT.com, and register. You will enjoy the consistent journey by learning through our **SAT Question of the Day.**

ANSWERS AND
EXPLANATIONS

READING AND WRITING MODULE 1

Directions: The questions in this section address a number of important reading and writing skills. Each question includes one or more passages, which may include a table or graph. Read each passage and question carefully, and then choose the best answer to the question based on the passage(s). All questions in this section are multiple-choice with four answer choices. Each question has a single best answer.

Brown University, a private Ivy League research university in Providence, Rhode Island, was established in 1764. At the time of its creation, Brown's charter was uniquely _____; while other colleges had curricular strictures against opposing doctrines, Brown's charter asserted, "Sectarian differences of opinions shall not make any Part of the Public and Classical instruction."

Which choice completes the text with the most logical and precise word or phrase?

A) orthodox
B) proverbial
C) progressive
D) controversial

Explanation

Brain Work: The blank is followed by a semi-colon, which implies that what comes after the punctuation mark is an explanation of what goes before it. The last part asserts that the charter asserted that sectarian differences of opinion shall not make any part of … instruction, but other universities had curricular restrictions (strictures) against opposing doctrines. This implies that the charter is 'broad-minded' and the correct option should reflect this.

Specifics:

Choice A: incorrect because if a charter is 'orthodox', it is not likely to be 'broad-minded'.

Choice B: incorrect because the word 'proverbial' means 'related to a proverb' or 'becoming a proverb or byword'. This sense is not supported by any phrase in the text.

Choice C: correct because if something is 'progressive', it is related to progress and thus, this word is the best fit in the context.

Choice D: incorrect because the word 'controversial' is not fit in the context because if sectarian differences are not part of instruction, it CANNOT be controversial.

Verdict:

Thus, the correct answer is Choice C.

<u>Question 2</u>

Spanish flue is a common misnomer for the 1918 flue pandemic whose fatality was estimated at 6 to 10 million in the United States alone. The pandemic broke out near the end of World War I, when wartime censors in belligerent countries suppressed bad news to maintain morale, but newspapers freely reported the outbreak in neutral Spain, creating _____ impression of Spain as the epicenter of the disease.

Which choice completes the text with the most logical and precise word or phrase?

A) a false
B) a threatening
C) a realistic
D) an unbiased

Explanation

Brain Work: The key phrase in the text is 'misnomer' (a wrong or inappropriate name). In belligerent (warring) countries, wartime censors suppressed the bad news (real numbers of deaths), but in neutral Spain, the outbreaks were freely reported, that is the number of deaths were accurately given in Spain. This created an impression that resulted in the 'misnomer'. Thus, the impression is 'not correct'. Thus, 'false' can be a logical word for the blank.

Specifics:

Choice A: correct as per the explanation given above.

Choice B: incorrect because if the impression is a 'threatening' impression, Spanish flue is not likely to be a misnomer.

Choice C: incorrect because if the impression is 'realistic', Spanish flue is not likely to be a misnomer.

Choice D: incorrect because if the impression is 'unbiased', then it will not result in a misnomer.

Verdict:

Thus, the correct answer is Choice A.

Question 3

Electroluminescence (the process of releasing light from electrons) from single molecules that form a thin layer on a semi-conductor imposes _____ demands for molecule-electrode coupling. To conduct electrons, the molecular orbitals need to be hybridized with electrodes. To emit light, they need to be decoupled from the electrodes to prevent the absorption of fluorescence.

Which choice completes the text with the most logical and precise word or phrase?

A) persistent
B) consequential
C) transient
D) inconsistent

Explanation

Brain work: The blank is present before a noun, giving a hint that a word describing the demands is needed in the blank. We need to look out for the clues in the light of this information. The second sentence says that to conduct electrons, the molecular orbitals are to be hybridized with electrodes and the third sentence says that they are to be decoupled from the electrodes. These two requirements are opposing each other. Thus, the word required for the blank should be with this sense. Thus, the correct answer is Choice D.

Specifics:

Choice A: incorrect because the word 'persistent' (which means stubborn or dogged) is not logically fit in the blank; there is no phrase in the text that supports the use of this word.

Choice B: incorrect because the word 'consequential' (which means significant) is not logically fit in the blank; note that no part of text justifies the use of this word.

Choice C: incorrect because the word 'transient' (which means 'temporary') is not fit in the blank.

Choice D: correct because the word 'inconsistent' (which means 'opposing') is logically fit because being coupled with electrodes and being decoupled with them are opposite demands.

Verdict:

Thus, the correct answer is Choice D.

Question 4

In 1784, some 130 years before Einstein proposed black holes, English astronomical pioneer John Michell _____ the existence of black holes, bodies so big that even light could not escape from them. Michell's wild guess depended on simplistic calculations that assumed that such a body might have the same density of the Sun. his calculations also concluded that 'dark star' would form when its diameter exceeds the Sun's by a factor of 500, making the star extremely small.

Which choice completes the text with the most logical and precise word or phrase?

  A) established
  B) refuted

C) recanted

D) surmised

Explanation

Brain Work: The key phrase is 'Michell's wild guess'. This phrase suggests that Michell made a wild guess about the existence of black holes and the blank should have a word that gives this sense. Of the given options, the word 'surmised' (which means 'a thought or idea based on scanty evidence' or 'conjecture') is the logical fit for the for the blank.

Specifics:

Choice A: incorrect because Michell did not prove that black holes exist.

Choice B: incorrect because the word 'refute' (which means 'disprove') is not logical in the context.

Choice C: incorrect because the word 'recant' (which means 'to withdraw a statement, often publicly') is not logical in the context.

Choice D: correct because the word 'surmised' is logically fit in the context as per the explanation given above.

Verdict:

Thus, the correct answer is Choice D.

Question 5

Based on her own experiences and her study of Native American cultures, Paula Gunn Allen wrote *The Sacred Hoop: Recovering the Feminine in American Indian Traditions* (1986). This ground-breaking work argued that the dominant cultural view of Native American societies was biased and that European explorers understood Native Peoples through the patriarchal lens. She _____ such views by describing the central role women played in many Native American cultures.

Which choice completes the text with the most logical and precise word or phrase?

A) underscored
B) undermined
C) protested
D) proclaimed

Explanation

Brain Work: By interpreting the first sentence, we understand that Allen was trying to 'recover the feminine in American Indian traditions.' The book argues that the dominant cultural view was biased (against women). Overall, she tries to 'disprove' such views by describing the central role played by women in Native American cultures. Thus, we can guess that the word required in the blank is 'disprove' or 'refute'.

Specifics:

Choice A: incorrect because the word 'underscore' means 'emphasize', a sense which is not logical in the context.

Choice B: correct because the word 'undermine' (which means 'weaken') is the logical fit for the blank.

Choice C: incorrect because, while the word 'protest' has the sense of 'fighting against' something publicly, we generally protest an injustice or an unjust law, not a view.

Choice D: incorrect because the word which has a positive connotation of support is not logical in the context.

Verdict:

Thus, the correct answer is Choice B.

Question 6

By definition, parasites are costly for their hosts as they _____ resources for their own growth, reproduction, and survival with no rewards for the hosts. Given the cost of parasitism, hosts are expected to evolve defense mechanisms aiming at limiting the negative effect of parasitism on their fitness. Consequently, hosts have evolved a series of morphological, physiological and behavioral adaptations to fight off parasitic attacks.

Which choice completes the text with the most logical and precise word or phrase?

A) squander
B) divert
C) optimize
D) manage

Explanation

Brain Work: By looking at the passage, we understand that parasitism is costly for hosts. This implies that parasites 'steal' resources from hosts. Thus, the word required in the blank should have a sense of 'stealing'. We should look at the options in the light of this information.

Specifics:

Choice A: incorrect because, though the word 'squander' (which means 'to waste') sounds correct in the context, this word is not logical because when parasites are using resources for their own growth, reproduction and survival, they don't 'waste' resources.

Choice B: correct because when they are diverting the resources for their own growth, they are using the resources that are to be used by hosts, and this phenomenon proves that parasitism is costly for hosts.

Choice C: incorrect because the word 'optimize' is not logically fit in the blank; by context, we need to use a negative word in the blank.

Choice D: incorrect because the word 'manage' is not logically fit in the blank.

Verdict:

Thus, the correct answer is Choice B.

<u>Question 7</u>

In the early 1960s, American computer scientist Paul Baran developed the concept that he called 'distributed adaptive message block switching', with a goal of providing 'safe' method for telecommunication of messages. His ideas contradicted the then-established principles of pre-allocation of network bandwidth, exemplified by the development of telecommunications in the Bell system. The new concept found little resonance among network implementers until the independent work of British computer scientist Donald Davies in 1965. Davies was credited with coining the modern term *packet switching*, a concept leading to development of ARPANET, the precursor network of the modern internet.

Which choice best states the main purpose of the text?

A) To bring out fundamental differences between two communication systems
B) To contrast the works of two computer scientists
C) To describe how the work of two scientists helped the origin of internet
D) To attribute the origin of internet to telecommunications

Explanation

Brain work: The passage introduces Paul Baran's work to provide a 'safe' method for communication of messages, which is different from the Bell system. Later, Davies worked on Baran's concept to develop packet switching, resulting in the precursor of internet. Thus, the main purpose of the passage is to discuss how the work of two scientists led to the development of internet. We should look at the options in the light of this information.

Specifics:

Choice A: incorrect because the passage does not discuss the fundamental differences between telecommunications and internet; though both of them are mentioned, the difference is a detail that constitutes a minor point of the passage.

Choice B: incorrect because the passage does not discuss the differences between Baran's work and Daves' work.

Choice C: correct because this option captures the essence of the passage.

Choice D: incorrect because the origin of internet is not connected to telecommunications; instead, the passage brings out the separate principles behind them – refer to the second sentence of the passage.

Verdict:

Thus, the correct answer is Choice C.

Question 8

The following text is adapted from Edgar Rice Burroughs' 1912 novel *A Princess of Mars*. John Carter, the protagonist, is narrating his thoughts.

> I have never told this story, nor shall mortal man see this manuscript until after I have passed over for eternity. I know that the average human mind will not believe what it cannot grasp. And so, I do not propose being pilloried by the public, and held up as a colossal liar when I am but telling the simple truths which some day science will substantiate. Possibly the suggestions which I gained from Mars, and the knowledge which can set down in this chronicle, will aid in an earlier

understanding of our sister planet; <u>mysteries to you, but no longer mysteries to me</u>.

Which choice best describes the function of the underlined part in the text as a whole?

A) It gives the rationale behind the claim made in the second sentence.

B) It gives an exception for the author's claim in the earlier sentence.

C) It justifies the author's hope that is suggested in the earlier sentence.

D) It gives the reason for the author's statement in the first sentence.

Explanation

Brain Work: This question is a rhetorical purpose question; we need to understand why the author uses this underlined part. To do this, we need to understand the context in which the author uses the sentence. By analyzing the passage, we understand that the narrator is saying that he is going to tell us something unbelievable and hopes that this will help an earlier understanding of Mars. The author uses the underlined part in this context. We should verify the options in the light of this information.

Specifics:

Choice A: the second sentence gives us the narrator's awareness that 'the average human mind will not believe what it cannot grasp. The underlined part does not give the reason for the concept given in the second sentence and hence, this option is incorrect.

Choice B: The sentence before the earlier part says that the author's knowledge will help scientists gain an earlier knowledge about Mars. The underlined part does not give the exception to this concept. Thus, this option is incorrect.

Choice C: The earlier sentence expresses the author's hope that his knowledge helps us have an earlier understanding of Mars. The underlined part gives the reason (that those mysteries are not mysteries to the narrator) for his hope mentioned in the earlier sentence. Thus, this is the correct option.

Choice D: The first sentence expresses the author's disinclination to write about the unbelievable things about Mars that are known to him. The underlined part is not the logical reason for that. Hence, this is the incorrect option.

Verdict:

Thus, the correct answer is Choice C.

Question 9

In Greek mythology, Pygmalion is a sculptor who loved his beautiful statue which he sculpted so much that it came to life. In an experiment popularly known as Pygmalion effect, psychologists Rosenthal and Jacobson informed faculty members of Oak Elementary School that some students, whose identifies were given to the teacher, had great academic potential. Unbeknown to the teachers, they were just randomly selected students. This resulted in a self-fulfilling prophesy where the teachers unconsciously focused their energies on the 'high-performing' students. These students were retested eight months later, and they did score significantly higher in the test.

Which choice best states the function of the underlined sentence in the overall structure of the text?

A) To draw a parallel between the teachers and the statue
B) To present a specific reason for the Pygmalion effect
C) To explain the importance of selection of students
D) To hint at the idea that the selected students did have great academic potential

Explanation

Brain Work: This question is a rhetorical purpose question; we need to identify the purpose served by the underlined part in the context of the passage. The passage first introduces a Greek myth, in which the sculptor loved the statue so much that it came to life. The Pygmalion effect in the experiment is that the teachers' belief that the students had high potential resulted in a better result in those selected students – note that the teachers' unconscious focus is the actual reason for their better performance. We need to verify each option in the light of this information.

Specifics:

Choice A: As per the comparison in the text, the teachers are compared to Pygmalion and the students to the statue. But his option says that the teachers are compared to the statue, a concept which is wrong. Thus, this option is incorrect.

Choice B: As per the comparison, students' better performance is the Pygmalion effect and the underlined sentence gives the reason for the effect. Hence, this option is correct.

Choice C: As per the passage, the students are randomly selected and so, the underlined portion does not talk about the importance of the random selection. Thus, this option is incorrect.

Choice D: The passage never mentions that the randomly selected students had great academic potential and thus, this option is incorrect.

Verdict:

Thus, the correct answer is Choice B.

The following text is from *Songs of Travel and Other Verses,* a 1908 poetry anthology written by Robert Louis Stevenson.

> Or let autumn fall on me
> Where I afield I linger,
> Silencing the bird on tree,
> Biting the blue finger;
> White as meal the frosty field -
> Warm the fireside haven -
> Not to autumn will I yield,
> Not to winter even!

Which choice best states the main purpose of the text?

A) To describe the woes caused to a traveler by the inclement weather

B) To call attention to the poet's persistence in the face of unforgiving seasons

C) To reminisce about the difficulties faced by a traveler

D) To depict the poet's indifference to difficulties due to his love for travel

Explanation

Brain Work:

Looking at the question, we understand that the question requires us to understand the overall purpose of the given poem. We understand that the poet cares only for 'lingering afield', not for the autumn silencing the birds, or for winter that makes his fingers blue. He is interested only in his travel, not in the difficulties caused by changing seasons. We can verify options in the light of this information.

Specifics:

Choice A: though the poem describes the difficulties caused by inclement weather, the main focus is on 'his not yielding'. Thus, this option gives the minor detail used in the poem and thus, this option is incorrect.

Choice B: though this option correctly brings out the author's persistence in the face of unforgiving seasons, his love for travel, which is the central concept of the poem, is not mentioned and thus, this option is incorrect.

Choice C: incorrect because the word 'reminisce' invokes past experience, while the author talks about future persistence (note the use of future in the last lines). Hence, this option is incorrect.

Choice D: correct because this option encapsulates the author's feelings comprehensively and thus, is the right option for this 'main idea' question.

Verdict:

Thus, the correct answer is Choice D.

Question 11

The following text is adapted from A Comedy of Masks, a novel by Ernest Dowson and Arthur Moore published in 1893. Rainham, a dock proprietor, was talking to an artist who uses the property for his painting work.

> He looked up with a smile, in which an onlooker might have detected a spark of malice. He was a slight man of middle height, and of no apparent distinction, and his face with all its petulant lines of lassitude and ill-health – the wear and tear of forty years having done with him the work of fifty – struck one who saw Philip Rainham for the first time by nothing so much as by his ugliness. And yet few persons who knew him would

have hesitated to allow to his nervous, suffering visage a certain indefinable charm.

According to the text, what is true about Rainham?

    A) He was almost always malicious.
    B) He was distinct from others in strange ways.
    C) He appeared older than he was.
    D) His sickly face looked grotesque to others.

Explanation

Brain Work: the use of 'according to...' implies that the question requires us to identify information directly given in the text. We need to understand the text and verify each option individually to find a piece of information that is correct as per the text. A careful reading makes us understand that the passage gives description of Rainham.

Specifics:

Choice A: the first sentence says an onlooker might have detected a spark of malice (in his smile), but it does not mean that he was always malicious; no information in the passage suggests this fact. Thus, this option is incorrect.

Choice B: the second sentence of the text says that he was a man of 'no distinction', implying that he was an ordinary man. Thus, this information is incorrect and so this option is incorrect.

Choice C: a part of the second sentence says that 'wear and tear of forty years having done with him the work of fifty'. This implies that he was forty, but his face looked fifty. Thus, this option is correct.

Choice D: the last sentence says that '...suffering visage a certain indefinable charm'. This implies that his sickly face did have some charm. Thus, this option is incorrect.

Verdict: Thus, the correct answer is Choice C.

"The Garden" is a 1913 poem written by Ezra Pound. In the poem, Pound describes the internal conflict felt by a rich woman, who happens to watch poor kids in a garden.

Which quotation from "The Garden" most effectively describes the conflict?

A) "And round about there is a rabble/ of filthy, sturdy, unkill-able infants of the very poor. / They shall inherit the earth."
B) "In her is the end of breeding. / Her boredom is exquisite and excessive."
C) "She would like someone to speak to her, / and is almost afraid that I / will commit that indiscretion."
D) "Like a skien of loose silk blown against a wall / She walks by the railing of a path in Kensington Gardens, / and she is dying piece-meal / of a sort of emotional anaemia."

Explanation

Brain Work: This is a question that requires us to identify evidence in support of the statement given in the text. As per the question, Pound describes the internal conflict and we need to identify an option that proves the internal conflict being described by Pound. We need to verify each option in the light of this information.

Specifics:

Choice A: these lines talk about the poor kids, and about the poet's hope that they will inherit the earth. But the lines do not talk about the internal conflict and thus, the option is not correct.

Choice B: these lines talk about her being the end of breeding and about her boredom. They don't talk about any internal conflict. So, this is not the correct option.

Choice C: the first line talks about her desire to talk to someone and the next two lines express her fear of being talked to. This reflects the internal conflict and so, this is the correct option.

Choice D: the first two lines talk about her walk in the garden, and the next two lines talk about her 'emotional death'. There is no internal conflict described in the lines and so, this is not the correct option.

Verdict:

Thus, the correct answer is Choice C.

Question 13

One of the founding fathers of Cubism, Albert Gleizes was in equal parts artist, theoretician, and philosopher and was responsible for bringing Cubism to the attention of the general public. However, some critics argue that Gleizes' art work took notable turn when, after his discharge from the army in 1915, he moved to New York where his work took on the frantic inspirations of life in that city.

Which of the following Gleizes' paintings would most directly support the critics' claim?

A) *Banks of the Marne* depicts a bright crimson sky that is pock-marked with purples and blues, making it a vigorous expression of the artist's subjectivity.
B) *Countryside* is a painting with his brushwork and also his choice of a single-perspective viewpoint reminisces some aspects of Impressionism.
C) *Woman with Phlox* stands as a revolutionary piece because it presents flattened forms and compressed space, depicting a seated woman staring down intently reading.
D) *Composition for "Jazz"* presents rudimentary elements of two performers both of whom are adorned in extravagant head-dress, a common attire of urban jazz players.

Explanation

Brain Work: the critics' stand is that Gleizes' work took on frantic inspiration of life in that city. We need to identify, from among the options, a painting that supports the critics' claim. Note that the first sentence is of just introductory nature, for it has nothing to do with the question we need to answer.

Specifics:

Choice A: this option describes the technicalities of his painting, but does not show that the painting stands proof for the urban influence. Hence this option is not the correct option.

Choice B: this option indicates the influence of Impressionism, but not the urban influence. Hence, this option is not correct.

Choice C: the option depicts the subject and technical description, but this information does not present the urban influence, which is essential for the correct option. Thus, this option is incorrect.

Choice D: this option the elements of the painting that are the result of his observation of urban setting, and thus, this option shows the urban influence on the painter. Thus, this option is correct.

Verdict: thus, the correct answer is Choice D.

Question 14

Extinction rates during different geological periods of the Earth.

Name of the geological	Date	Intensity of extinction
Ordovician	- Ended 443 MYA	- 57% of genera lost - 86% of species lost
Late Devonian	- Ended 359 MYA	- 35% of genera lost. - 75% of species lost
Permian-Triassic	- Ended 251 MYA	- 56% genera lost - 96% of species lost
Triassic-Jurassic	- Ended 200 MYA	- 47% of genera lost - 80% of species lost

*MYA – Million Years Ago

Some researchers studying the major extinction episodes that happened on Earth have paid attention to the first four extinction episodes out of all the five major extinction episodes earth has faced; Ordovician, Late Devonian, Permian-Triassic, and Triassic-Jurassic periods. In fact, extinction figures given are merely estimates that have been arrived at by using fossil records. Basing on the information, they can conclusively conclude that _____.

Which choice most effectively uses data from the table to complete the argument?

A) Ordovician extinction resulted in loss of higher number of species than did Permian-Triassic extinction

B) highest number of species were lost during Permian-Triassic extinction

C) lowest proportion of genera were lost during Triassic-Jurassic extinction

D) after the four extinctions, most of the species were lost

Explanation

Brain Work:

To answer this type of question that requires you to identify a correct statement from among the options, it is not advisable time to spend time on studying the data. Pay attention to the question and understand how to verify each option in the light of information given in the argument and in the data.

Choice A: as per the data, Ordovician extinction resulted in loss of 86% of species and Permian-Triassic extinction lost 96% of species. However, the option might be correct or incorrect because the option talks about number of species while data contain information in percentages. We cannot conclusively say whether the option is correct or incorrect. Thus, this option is incorrect.

Choice B: the data state that Permian-Triassic extinction lost 96% of species, but percentage cannot be equated to actual numbers, and thus, this option may be correct or may be incorrect. Thus, this option is incorrect.

Choice C: if we consider proportion, lowest proportion implies lowest percentage. If we compare the percentages, the lowest proportion of genera is lost during Late Devonian, and thus, this information is incorrect.

Choice D: if we consider the cumulative effect, most of the species have been lost after the four extinction episodes. Thus, this option is correct.

Verdict:

Thus, the correct answer is Choice D.

Question 15

Species	hybrid zone		non-hybrid zone	
	Intra-specific reproduction	Inter-specific reproduction	Intra-specific reproduction	Inter-specific reproduction
Sphyrapicus ruber	72%	28%	89%	11%
Sphyrapicus nuchalis	86%	14%	94%	6%

James Smith and Patricia Anderson recently studied the frequency of inter-specific and intra-specific reproductions in two species of sapsuckers: red-breasted sapsucker (*Sphyrapicus ruber*) and red-naped sapsucker (*Sphyrapicus nuchalis*). Both these species of sapsuckers show more frequent inter-specific reproduction than all other species of sapsuckers. It is a proven fact that the chance of inter-specific reproduction is more in a hybrid zone than in a non-hybrid zone. The biologists also studied genetic diversity of both species in both the zones. Basing on their study, they concluded that genetic diversity is more pronounced in cases of reproduction when it happens inter-specifically than when it happens intra-specifically.

Which choice states an observation that, in combination with data from the table, best supports the researchers' conclusion?

A) The genetic diversity of both species is higher in hybrid zone than that in non-hybrid zone.
B) The genetic diversity of *S. nuchalis* in hybrid zone is more than that of *S. ruber* in hybrid zone.
C) The genetic diversity of *S. ruber* in non-hybrid zone is more than that of *S. ruber* in hybrid zone.
D) The genetic diversity of *S. nuchalis* in hybrid zone is less that in non-hybrid zone.

Explanation

Brain Work:

The overall conclusion is that genetic diversity is more in cases of reproduction when it happens inter-specifically than when it happens intra-specifically. We need to support this conclusion in the light of data given in the table. The observation given in the answer option should support the conclusion when the observation is used in conjunction with the data.

Specifics:

Choice A: the data shows that inter-specific reproduction is more frequent for both species in hybrid zones than it is in non-hybrid zones. In addition to this, if genetic diversity is more in hybrid zones than in non-hybrid zones, it is proven that inter-specific reproduction is the reason for genetic diversity. Thus, this is the correct option.

Choice B: the comparison of genetic diversity between different species, as is given in this option, cannot be relevant to the conclusion and thus, this option is not correct.

Choice C: this information actually argues against the conclusion and thus, this is not the correct option.

Choice D: this information too argues against the conclusion and so, this is not the correct option.

Verdict:

Thus, the correct answer is Choice A.

Question 16

Prorocentrum cf. *balticum* is a microbe which can eat other microbes and can also prepare its food in photosynthesis. Biologists Michaela Larsson and Martina Doblin, who recently discovered this microbe, observed that this microbe can create a carbon sink that naturally removes carbon, which is the major reason for global warming. Having capacity to acquire nutrients in different ways means that this microbe can occupy parts of the ocean devoid of dissolved nutrients and therefore unsuitable for most phytoplankton. The biologists hypothesize that the existence of this microbe in such ocean parts will help oceans act as better natural carbon sink, when the effects of global warming become more pronounced in the future.

Which finding, if true, would most directly support the biologists' hypothesis?

A) *Prorocentrum* cf. *balticum* voraciously feeds on other phytoplankton that are currently present in ocean parts devoid of dissolved nutrients.

B) *Prorocentrum* cf. *balticum* can sequester carbon, even as oceans become more acidic due to global warming.

C) Currently, *Prorocentrum* cf. *balticum* contributes only to a tiny portion of carbon sequestration happening in ocean due to other phytoplankton.

D) Other species of phytoplankton act as carbon sinks because they remove carbon from circulation due to their metabolic processes.

Explanation

Brain Work:

By studying the argument, we can understand that *Prorocentrum* cf. *balticum* removes carbon, thereby helping us fight global warming. Their hypothesis is this microbe will make oceans better carbon sink. We need to identify a piece of evidence that supports this hypothesis.

Specifics:

Choice A: if the microbe voraciously feed on other phytoplankton, which helps us remove carbon, then the existence of the microbe will have adverse impact on carbon sequestering ability of ocean. Thus, this option actually weakens the biologists' hypothesis. Thus, this is incorrect.

Choice B: if this microbe can sequester even when the oceans become more acidic due to global warming, then it is likely to make oceans better carbon sinks. This gives direct support to the hypothesis and thus, is the correct option.

Choice C: this information adds to current carbon-sequestering capacity of oceans, not to the future oceans' ability. Thus, this information is not relevant to the hypothesis and thus, this option is not the correct option.

Choice D: this option gives information about other phytoplankton and thus, is not relevant to the hypothesis which is about *Prorocentrum* cf. *balticum*. Hence, it is not the correct option.

Verdict:

Thus, Choice B is the correct answer.

Question 17

Worldwide environmental change resulting from the impact of a large celestial object with earth and/or from vast volcanic eruptions is commonly believed to be the reason for the extinction of dinosaurs at the boundary between Cretaceous and Paleogene eras, about 66 million years ago. However, there exists certain geological and paleontological evidence, such as the fossils showing their decline even during the Mesozoic era (252 million to 66 million years ago), the geological proof that different dinosaur species evolved rapidly and were quickly replaced by others throughout the Mesozoic and evidence that extant birds are theropod dinosaurs' lineage, proving that _____.

Which choice most logically completes the text?

A) the catastrophic event commonly believed to be the cause for the extinction was not the reason for the extinction of any dinosaur species

B) many factors other than the catastrophic event were responsible for the sudden disappearance of dinosaur species

C) many species other than dinosaurs became extinct in the aftermath of the catastrophic event

D) neither the purported extinction event was complete nor the catastrophic event was the sole cause for it

Explanation

Brain Work:

The first sentence states the popular belief that a particular catastrophic event was the reason for the extinction of dinosaurs. The following sentence casts doubt by giving out some geological and paleontological evidence – note the use of the transition marker 'however'. By analyzing the whole sentence, we understand that we need to draw a conclusion basing on the different pieces of evidence given. The whole argument seeks to prove that the belief is wrong. We should select the correct option in the light of this information.

Specifics:

Choice A: This information does not consider all pieces of evidence given in the second sentence of the argument. While some dinosaurs did become extinct, some other species were not. This concept is not included in this option and thus, this option is incorrect.

Choice B: The argument does not present any factors other than the catastrophic event described. Moreover, this option does not consider the issue of extant birds. Thus, the option is incorrect.

Choice C: the argument does not contain any information about the extinction of other species and thus, this option is incorrect.

Choice D: this option draws a conclusion that depends on all pieces of evidence given. Thus, this is the correct option.

Verdict: Thus, the correct answer is Choice D.

Question 18

A social construct is a concept that exists not in objective reality, but as a result of human interaction. It exists because humans agree that it exists. The concept that one person can 'murder' another person or one 'infringes on' the right of the other is a social construct, while 'killing' or 'snatching' an article from the other is a reality independent of human interaction or mutual human agreement. In legal proceedings, therefore, _____.

Which choice most logically completes the text?

A) judiciary seeks to judge the conflicting sides basing on the existence of the social construct, rather than on the legal merit
B) existence of social construct is an essentiality rather than a supplement, for law itself is a social construct
C) judgments are construed as valid and fair decisions depending only on the legal validity of the arguments presented by both sides

D) objective reality becomes the basis for offering judgments, regardless of subjective interpretations

Explanation

Brain Work:

The first sentences of the text introduce a social construct and the last sentence seeks to connect this concept of social construct to legal proceedings. We need to identify how social constructs are at work in legal proceedings. We should verify the options in the light of this information.

Specifics:

Choice A: this option does relate the social construct to legal proceedings. It, however, undermines the legal merit, giving the sense that judiciary judges 'without' considering the legal merit. This is not logical and thus, this option is incorrect.

Choice B: this option relates the social construct by concluding that it is an essential feature in legal proceedings. Thus, this is the correct option.

Choice C: this option considers only legal validity, implying that social constructs are not needed in judicial proceedings. This sense is not logical and thus, this option is not correct.

Choice D: this option totally ignores the concept of social construct, making this information irrelevant in the whole context. Thus, this option is incorrect.

Verdict:

Thus, the correct answer is Choice B.

Question 19

Designing effective conservation strategies must consider the location-specific needs of people who depend on forests for their livelihood. However, policy makers usually find _____ to be quite a challenging process, primarily because accurate information about the efficacy of strategies implemented in the past is rarely available.

Which choice completes the text so that it conforms to the conventions of Standard English?

   A) them
   B) theirs
   C) its
   D) it

Explanation

Brain Work:

Looking at the options, we understand that we need to select a correct pronoun, which is to agree with the logical noun. By studying the concept, we understand that the pronoun in the blank should logically refer to the process of 'designing effective conservation strategies' – we can understand this by observing the following now 'a challenging process'.

Specifics:

Choice A: the plural pronoun 'them' cannot refer to the singular antecedent 'designing…'. Thus, this option is incorrect.

Choice B: the plural form 'theirs' cannot logically agree in number with the singular antecedent.

Choice C: the word 'its', which is the possessive form of 'it', is not grammatically correct in the blank.

Choice D: the pronoun 'it' agrees in number with the singular antecedent 'designing …strategies'. Note that the 'ing' form acting as subject is to be taken as a singular noun and thus, the singular pronoun 'it' agrees with the antecedent.

Verdict:

The correct answer is Choice D.

Question 20

Traditionally, most boomerangs used by Aboriginal groups in Australia were non-returning. These weapons, sometimes called kylies, were used for hunting a variety of prey, from kangaroos to <u>parrots; at</u> a range of about 100 meters, a 2-kg non-returning boomerang could inflict mortal injury to a large animal.

A) parrots; at
B) parrots, at
C) parrots. at
D) parrots at

Explanation

Brain work:

When we are to answer this type of question that tests punctuation, we need to understand how the phrases and clauses are inter-related. The second sentence is with the main clause ("These weapons..."). The modifier prepositional phrase ("from Kangaroos to parrots") is related to the earlier main clause and is connected to the phrase by a comma. Another prepositional phrase ("at a range of ... meters") is connected to the next main clause ("a 2-kg... large animal"). Both the second and the third sentences are conceptually closely connected because the second sentence says that kylies were used for hunting and the third sentence describes how effective it was used for hunting. Thus, the third sentence is an explanation of the second sentence.

111

Specifics:

Choice A: this option correctly uses a semi-colon to connect two main clauses that are closely related. The last sentence exemplifies the concept present in the earlier sentence. Thus, they are correctly connected by a semicolon. This sentence is correct.

Choice B: this option uses a comma to connect two main clause and a comma cannot be used this way. This results in a run-on sentence. This is an error and thus, this option is incorrect.

Choice C: Though the option aptly separates two main clauses by using a period, this option is not preferable because two closely related sentences are separated by a period. Moreover, the new sentence has to begin with a capital letter, which is not used. Thus, this sentence is incorrect.

Choice D: the two main clauses are not connected by any punctuation, making this option incorrect.

Verdict: thus, Choice A is the correct answer.

Question 21

In 1894, Maris Sklodowska (or Madam Curie, as she would be known as later) visited her family in Poland and was still labouring under the illusion that she would be able to work in her chosen field in Poland. However, she was denied a place by the male professors at Krakow University, though her qualifications were no less than _____, primarily because of sexism in academia.

Which choice completes the text so that it conforms to the conventions of Standard English?

   A) them
   B) they're
   C) their
   D) theirs

Explanation

Brain work:

By studying the sentence and by observing the options, we understand that the point being tested is related to pronoun and its correct form. The subordinate clause with the blank contains a comparison and the comparison is between her qualifications and the male professors' qualifications. Correct option should express this comparison.

Specifics:

Choice A: this option uses the pronoun 'them', referring to the 'male professors'. In such a case, the comparison becomes faulty because 'her qualifications' cannot logically be compared to 'them'.

Choice B: this option contains the phrase referring to male professors, making the comparison faulty. Thus, this option is incorrect.

Choice C: this option contains the determiner 'their' which needs to be followed by the relevant noun to be grammatically correct. Thus, this option is incorrect.

Choice D: this option uses the possessive pronoun (theirs), correctly suggesting 'their qualifications'. Thus, this option is correct.

Verdict:

Thus, the correct answer is Choice D.

Question 22

Specifically referencing modern social media sites such as Facebook and Twitter, Eden Litt and Eszter Hargittai explain that the term *imagined audience* refers to a mental construct people form of their _____ who is actually consuming their online content.

Which choice completes the text so that it conforms to the conventions of Standard English?

A) audience, without real insight into,

B) audience without real insight into

C) audience; without real insight into

D) audience, without insight into

Explanation

Brain Work:

By studying the context, we understand that the question tests punctuation principles. We understand that additional information is usually demarcated from the rest of the sentences with a set of commas on either side. By interpreting the sentence, we can infer that the underlined part is a part of definition and so no part of the sentence can be considered additional information.

Brian Work:

Choice A: the use of commas implies that the information between commas is non-essential information, but the preposition phrase ("without real insight into") is essential information and so use of commas is incorrect.

Choice B: the absence of commas with the prepositional phrase ("without real insight ... online content") becomes essential information, satisfying the need of the context. Thus, this is the correct option.

Choice C: the use of semicolon requires a main clause after it, but the part present after it ("without real ... online content") is a sentence fragment, which is rhetorically not acceptable in Standard English. Thus, this option is incorrect.

Choice D: the use of comma makes the whole prepositional phrase ("without insight... online content") additional information and thus this option is incorrect.

Verdict:

Thus, the correct answer is Choice B.

Question 23

The Great Depression (1929-1939) was an economic shock that impacted most countries across the world, resulting in economic disasters in almost all the countries in the world and Germany, which was already suffering in the aftermath of World War I, was no exception. The financial crisis there escalated out of control in mid-1931, _____ with the collapse of the Credit Anstalt, a major German bank, in Vienna in May.

Which choice completes the text so that it conforms to the conventions of Standard English?

A) started
B) being started
C) starting
D) to start

Explanation

Brain Work:

By studying the sentence, we understand that the sentence with the blank is describing the financial crisis in Germany in the context of the Great Depression. The financial crisis started with the collapse of the German bank in May and escalated out of control in mid-1931. We need to select the correct answer option that effectively expresses this idea, while conforming to the conventions of Standard English.

Specifics:

Choice A: if we use the main verb 'started', we need to use a conjunction 'and' to make it grammatically correct. The correction, however, remains illogical because a crisis escalating first and then starting is not chronologically acceptable in the context.

Choice B: the use of 'being started' implies continuity and the continuity of the action of 'starting' something is not logical.

Choice C: the use of participle after the comma gives the required logical sense. Thus, this option is correct.

Choice D: the use of to infinitive (to start) is not logical in the sense, because some crisis does not escalate 'to start itself'.

Verdict:

Thus, the correct answer is Choice C.

Fun Fact:

The use of comma with a participle has some implications that may radically change the meaning. Study the following example.

I talked to the students coming out of the class. (It was the students who were coming out the class.)

I talked to the students, coming out of the class. (It was I who was coming out the class.)

Note that, in this context, if comma is used, the participle phrase ("coming out of the class") modifies the subject 'I' and if comma is not used, the same participle phrase modifies the noun immediately before the phrase.

Question 24

Migratory birds inherit from their parents the directions in which they need to migrate in the autumn and spring. If the parents each have a different genetically encoded directions, their offspring will end up with an intermediate _____ if a southwest-migrating bird is crossed with a southeast-migrating bird, their offspring will head south when the time comes.

Which choice completes the text so that it conforms to the conventions of Standard English?

A) direction,
B) direction:

C) direction.

D) direction

Explanation

Brain work:

By studying the text given, we understand that, after the blank we have complete sentence and before the blank, we have another. If we study both sentences, we understand that the second sentence is explanation of what goes before. We need to verify the options with this information in mind.

Specifics:

Choice A: incorrect because the use of comma after the first sentence results in comma splice, an error of combining two sentences with a comma, rather than with a conjunction. Thus, this option is incorrect.

Choice B: this option uses a colon correctly; the sentence that follows the colon is an explanation of the sentence before it. This correct use of punctuation makes this option correct.

Choice C: incorrect because using a period is incorrect because the second sentence is an explanation of what goes before in the earlier sentence. Note that we need to use a capital letter after the period but a lower-case letter is used in the following sentence, making the sentence incorrect.

Choice D: incorrect because absence of any conjunction results in a run-on sentence, which is not acceptable in Standard English.

Verdict:

Thus, the correct answer is Choice B.

Question 25

Deep-sea fish live in regions where there is no natural illumination. Many of these are blind and rely on other senses, such as sensitivities to changes in local pressure and smell, to catch food and protect _____ from predators.

Which choice completes the text so that it conforms to the conventions of Standard English?

A) itself
B) it
C) themselves
D) them

Explanation

Brain Work:

By having a glance at the options, we understand that the question tests the conventions of use of correct pronoun and correct pronoun form. In the first place, we need to use a plural pronoun, because the pronoun in the blank needs to refer to 'many of these (deep-sea fish)' and we need to use the reflexive pronoun because the subject and object are one and the same.

Choice A: the pronoun 'itself', though a reflexive pronoun, cannot be used to refer to the plural antecedent – we know that the pronoun used should agree with the plural antecedent (here 'many of these') in number. Thus, this option is incorrect.

Choice B: the pronoun 'it' does not agree with the plural antecedent, and moreover, a reflexive pronoun is needed in the context. Thus, this sentence is incorrect.

Choice C: the pronoun 'themselves' is the correct reflexive form needed in the blank and it agrees with the plural antecedent. Thus, this option is incorrect.

Choice D: though a plural pronoun is correctly used, a reflexive pronoun that is needed in the context is not used, making this option incorrect.

Verdict:

Thus, the correct answer is Choice C.

Question 26

Endeavors with political and social ramifications beyond the playing field, many Native American games are seldom activities of frivolity and leisure. They can provide opportunities for expressions of cultural values and _____ other traditional activities, and thus, they can radiate potent symbolic meanings for participants and observers.

Which choice completes the text so that it conforms to the conventions of Standard English?

    A) incorporating
    B) incorporates
    C) may incorporate
    D) to incorporate

Explanation

Brain Work:

The first sentence declares that Native American games are not activities of frivolity and leisure. The second sentence contains a final part that discusses the result of 'reasons' given in the earlier part. We need to understand that the use of 'and' before the blank requires parallel elements. We need to verify options in the light of all this information.

Specifics:

Choice A: use of 'incorporating' results in incomplete sentence. This option can be found fault with on another ground as well; the use of 'ing' form after the conjunction 'and' requires another parallel 'ing' form before the 'and'. As no such parallel form is present earlier, this option is incorrect.

Choice B: the singular verb 'incorporates' does not agree with the plural subject 'they' and thus, this option is incorrect.

Choice C: the verb 'may incorporate' is parallel with 'can provide' and these two main clauses correctly give reasons for the final part 'thus, they can... observers'. This construction maintains parallel structure and correct logical flow in the whole text. Thus, this is the correct option.

Choice D: incorrect because the to infinitive 'to incorporate' has no parallel element in the earlier part and thus, this option is incorrect.

Verdict: Thus, the correct answer is Choice C.

Question 27

In the past two decades, our understanding of the physiological feats that enable migratory birds to cross immense oceans, fly above the highest mountains, or remain in unbroken flight for months at a stretch, has _____ birds continually exceed what we think are the limits of physical endurance, like a six-inch sandpiper weighing less than an ounce flying 3,300 miles nonstop for six days from Canadian subarctic to South America.

Which choice completes the text so that it conforms to the conventions of Standard English?

    A) been exploded, migrant
    B) exploded. Migrant
    C) exploded; migrant
    D) exploded: migrant

Explanation

Brain work:

The first main clause tells us how our understanding of bird migration has increased and the second part describes how migrant birds exceed what we think of limits of endurance. The final part gives an example of migrant birds' exceeding the limits of physical endurance, which is discussed in the second part of the text. We need to verify the options in the light of this information.

Specifics:

Choice A: the use of passive construction is problematic in this option; the use of active construction (our understanding ...has exploded) is logical, but the use of passive construction (our understanding ... has been exploded) gives illogical sense. Moreover, the use of comma results in comma splice error, which is not acceptable in Standard English. Thus, this option is incorrect.

Choice B: the period used after 'exploded' completes this sentence and the next sentence discusses another topic related to the concept given in the first sentence. Thus, this is the most logical construction that can be used in this context. Thus, this is the correct option.

Choice C: the use of semicolon is incorrect because the two concepts given by the clause after it and by the clause going before it are not closely related. Though they are talking about the same topic, the two sentences are not with concept that are close enough to be connected by a semicolon.

Choice D: the use of colon is incorrect because of the same reason as given for option C. Thus, this option is incorrect.

Verdict:

Thus, the correct answer is Choice B.

The American Civil War was among the first wars to utilize industrial warfare. Railroads, the telegraph, steamships, the ironclad warship, and mass-produced weapons were all widely used during the War. Resulting in around 700,000 deaths in soldiers, along with an undetermined number of civilian casualties, _____ making it the deadliest military conflict in American history.

Which choice completes the text so that it conforms to the conventions of Standard English?

A) the Civil War resulted in carnage,
B) the carnage of the Civil War resulted,
C) the Civil War's carnage was resulted,
D) it was the Civil War whose carnage was resulted,

Explanation

Brain Work:

The first two sentences describe the Civil War, and the last sentence gives the death toll resulting from the war. The initial modifier phrase ("Resulting in around ... casualties") should logically describe the subject that follows the modifier phrase. We should look at the options in the light of this information.

Specifics:

Choice A: the initial modifier phrase ("Resulting in around ... casualties") correctly modifies the subject ("The Civil War") and so, this option is grammatically correct.

Choice B: the initial modifier phrase ("Resulting in around ... casualties") does not logically result in carnage, because 'carnage is itself the mass-killing' and thus, it cannot result in death of 700,000 soldiers.

Choice C: incorrect because the initial modifier phrase ("Resulting in around ... casualties") does not modify the subject '(the Civil War's) carnage.'

Choice D: incorrect because of the same reason.

Verdict:

Thus, the correct answer is Choice A.

Fun Fact:

When the initial modifier phrase does not logically modify the subject, an error called 'dangling modifier' is resulted. Sometimes, this error may result in illogical or even absurd meanings. Study the following example.

Example:

Looking out of the window, a big tree can be seen.

(A big tree is looking out the window! This sense is absurd, right?)

Look at the corrected sentence: Looking out of the window, I/you/someone can see a big tree.

Question 29

While there has been a lot of research on solar and nuclear energy as Martian energy sources, nuclear power harbours potential human risks and current models of solar systems lack the energy storage capability to compensate for day/night and seasonal variations in generation. It is, _____, prudent to consider an alternative source such as wind for stable power generation.

Which choice completes the text with the most logical transition?

   A) above all,
   B) on the other hand
   C) consequently,
   D) for instance

Explanation

Brain Work:

To answer this kind of question, we need to understand the logical relation between this sentence and the other sentences. In the earlier sentence, two power sources that can be used on Mars are mentioned and the problems with both types of power sources are mentioned. The last sentence comments that it is wise to find an alternative source. This need to search for the alternatives is the result of the problems mentioned in the earlier sentence. We need to verify the options in the light of this information.

Specifics:

Choice A: the transition indicator 'above all' indicates that the concept mentioned after this phrase is more important than the concepts mentioned in the earlier part of the text. This is not the case in the given text and thus, this option is incorrect.

Choice B: we use 'on the other hand' to introduce the second of the two contrasting points, facts or ways of looking at something. This is not the case in the given text and thus, this option is incorrect.

Choice C: we use 'consequently' to indicate that the following is the consequence/result of what goes earlier. This is the logical case with the given context and thus, this is the correct option.

Choice D: we use 'for instance' to exemplify what goes in the earlier part of the sentence. This is not the case with the text given. Thus, this option is incorrect.

Verdict:

Thus, the correct answer is Choice C.

Domesticating animals was difficult work for the ancient man. The easiest animals to domesticate were herbivores that graze on vegetation, because they were easiest to feed: they did not need humans to kill other animals to feed them, or to grow special crops. Cows, _____ were easily domesticated. Herbivores that eat grains were more difficult to domesticate than herbivores that graze because grains were valuable and also needed to be domesticated.

Which choice completes the text with the most logical transition?

A) similarly,
B) for instance,
C) coincidentally,
D) furthermore,

Explanation

Brain Work:

The first sentence comments on the difficulty of domesticating animals. The second sentence talks about animals that were easiest to domesticate and about the reasons for the ease of that domestication. The third sentence, which contains the blank, states that cows were the easy to domesticate. Thus, this sentence gives the exemplification of the concept described in the second sentence. The last sentence, of course, talks about animals that were difficult to domesticate. We need to keep this information in mind when we verify the options.

Specifics:

Choice A: the use of 'similarly' in this sentence needs an example of another easily domesticated animal in the earlier sentence. Since such example is not given in the earlier sentence, use of 'similarly' is not logical in this sentence.

Choice B: the use of 'for instance' indicates exemplification; the sentence with the blank contains exemplification of concept present in the earlier sentence and thus, this is the correct option.

Choice C: the use of 'coincidentally' when we want to draw the readers' attention to a coincidence. As there is not any coincidence implied or stated, the use of 'coincidentally' is incorrect.

Choice D: we use 'furthermore' to introduce a piece of information or opinion that adds to the previous one. As no such instance is present in the context, use of 'furthermore' is not logical.

Verdict:

Thus, the correct answer is Choice B.

Question 31

In Europe, alchemy led to the discovery of manufacture of amalgams and advances in many other chemical processes. _____ by the 16th century, the alchemists in Europe had separated into two groups. The first focussed on the discovery of new compounds, leading to what is now Chemistry. The second continued to look at the more spiritual, metaphysical side of alchemy, continuing the search for immortality and the transmutation of base metals into gold.

Which choice completes the text with the most logical transition?

A) Ironically,
B) Eventually,
C) Surprisingly,
D) Additionally,

Explanation

Brain Work:

The first sentence introduces the effect of alchemy. The second talks about its separation into two groups. The last two sentences talk about two different branches of alchemy that resulted from the single branch of alchemy. We need to keep this information in mind to evaluate the options given.

Specifics:

Choice A: we use 'ironically' to draw attention to a situation that is odd because it involves a contrast (usually from common expectation). As the second sentence does not present any such 'oddity' in the context of the situation present in the first sentence, the use of 'ironically' is not justified in the blank.

Choice B: we use the adverb 'eventually' to mean 'in the end', especially when something has involved a long time. This context in which the blank is present justifies the use of 'eventually', making this option correct.

Choice C: we use the adverb 'surprisingly' when there is an element of surprise. Either the sentence before the blank or the ones after the blank do not present any element of surprise. Thus, this option is not fit in the blank

Choice D: we use 'additionally' to add a new element or concept in continuation to the one given before. We do not find such inference in the context and thus, this option is incorrect.

Verdict: Thus, the correct answer is Choice B.

While researching a topic, a student has taken the following notes:

- Chronic mountain sickness (CMS) typically develops after extended time living at high altitude of over 3,000 metres (9,800 ft).
- In 1925, CMS was first discovered by Carlos Monge Medrano, who specialised in diseases of high altitude.
- While 28% people residing permanently at high altitudes develop CMS, around 14% of visitors to these areas develop this condition after two years of high-altitude life.
- Recent genetic research shows that 98% of people who become victims of CMS show ANP32D gene.
- Basing on these observations, scientists have concluded that a particular gene makes people more vulnerable.

The student wants to present the research and its findings. Which choice most effectively uses relevant information from the notes to accomplish this goal?

A) The focus of the recent genetic research was on the medical condition CMS, which was originally described by Carlos Monge Medrano way back in 1925.

B) The genetic research has identified a particular gene that is the primary cause for CMS, which is commonly found in people residing at high altitude regions.

C) While CMS, a medical condition first described by Carlos Monge Medrano, may be caused by high-altitude life, recent research has showed that a specific gene increases people's susceptibility to it.

D) Recent research has identified that a particular genetic abnormality is the reason for CMS, which is caused primarily in people living at high altitudes.

Explanation

Brain Work:

To answer this type of question, we need to understand the information given in the notes, identify major ideas and minor ones, and select the option that presents major information without distorting the information. The description of the disease, its identification history, and the implications of recent research have been given.

Specifics:

Choice A: this option just mentions the focus of the recent research, without focusing on the conclusions drawn at the end. Thus, this option is incorrect.

Choice B: this option states that a particular gene is the primary cause, a statement that is not justified because life in high altitude is likely to be the primary cause for the medical condition.

Choice C: this option encapsulates all the information present in the notes and thus, is the best option.

Choice D: this option mentions genetic abnormality, which is not mentioned in the original notes. Thus, this option is incorrect.

Verdict:

Thus, the correct answer is Choice D.

Question 33

While researching a topic, a student has taken the following notes:

- Slave narratives, the narratives of ex-slaves, were personal accounts of what it was like to live in slavery.
- They also provided Northerners and the world a glimpse into the life of slave communities.
- They provide the most powerful voices contradicting the slaveholders' favourable claims concerning slavery, becoming the abolitionist movement's voice of reality.
- On the other hand, Harlem Renaissance, a cultural movement taking place from 1919 into 1930s, represented and gave voice to the African American thought.
- Unlike the stereotypes of description of suffering in Slave Narratives, Harlem Renaissance celebrated black identity, depicting their racial pride.
- It paved the way for the civil rights movement.

The student wants to comment on the objectives of slave narratives and Harlem Renaissance literature in relation to African Americans. Which choice most effectively uses relevant information from the notes to accomplish this goal?

A) The former depicted physical suffering caused by slavery before emancipation and the latter depicted intellectual trauma caused by racial discrimination after abolition.
B) The former paved the way for emancipation by enlightening the world about suffering, and the latter paved the way for spiritual emancipation, and the quest for equality of rights as well.
C) The former led to constitutional remedy to the evil of slavery, and the latter depicted the intellectual turmoil in the aftermath of the evil of slavery.
D) The former paved the way for political rights, while the latter paved the way for civil rights.

Explanation

Brain Work:

We need to understand what the question is asking for; we need to identify the 'objectives' of both literary genres. The first supported abolitionist movement leading to emancipation and the latter supported upliftment of pride about the black race and also civil rights movement. We need to look at the options, in the light of this information.

Specifics:

Choice A: the option depicts the nature of slave narratives, not its objectives. Moreover, Harlem Renaissance literature celebrates the pride of being 'black', not the intellectual trauma. Thus, this option is incorrect.

Choice B: this option correctly captures the essence of information given in the notes. Thus, this is the correct option.

Choice C: while this option correctly captures the essence of slave narratives, it does not describe the characteristic features of Harlem Renaissance literature.

Choice D: while this option correctly captures the essence Harlem renaissance literature, it does not depict the objective of slave narratives correctly – note that slave narratives were not aimed at political rights.

Verdict:

Thus, the correct answer is Choice B.

A small request from the authors

If you find this book useful, your feedback encourages us and so don't forget to give feedback on Amazon.com or whatever website you have downloaded this book from.

If you want regular practice with new questions, consider visiting our website www.RRDigitalSAT.com, and register. You will enjoy the consistent journey by learning through our **SAT Question of the Day.**

READING AND WRITING MODULE 2

Directions: The questions in this section address a number of important reading and writing skills. Each question includes one or more passages, which may include a table or graph. Read each passage and question carefully, and then choose the best answer to the question based on the passage(s). All questions in this section are multiple-choice with four answer choices. Each question has a single best answer.

Question 1

The genesis of the American Civil War is obvious. Under Abraham Lincoln's leadership, the war was fought to preserve the Union. With slavery so deeply _____, Union leaders by 1862 had reached the decision that slavery had to end in order for the Union to be restored. Union war evolved as the war progressed in response to political and military issues.

Which choice completes the text with the most logical and precise word or phrase?

    A) emotional
    B) entrenched
    C) divisive
    D) involved

Explanation

Brain Work:

The text talks about the genesis and evolution of the War. The sentence with the blank posits that leader decided to end the slavery in order to restore the Union. This implies that the slavery was the reason for the war. This implication can be understood because of the use of the modifier phrase ("With slavery... ,) because such initial modifier phrase generally hint at the reason for the observation found in the main clause. Thus, the word in the blank should hint at the idea that 'slavery was the reason for the War'. We should look at the options in the light of this information.

Specifics:

Choice A: if slavery was 'emotional', it might not result in a war, posing a danger to the Union. Thus, this is not the correct option.

Choice B: if slavery was deeply 'entrenched', it would be likely to continue; thus, this option does not give the intended sense in the blank.

Choice C: if slavery was deeply 'divisive', then it might result in a war. Thus, this option gives the required logical sense and so, this is the correct option.

Choice D: slavery being deeply involved could not be the reason for the war. Thus, this cannot be the correct option.

Verdict:

Thus, the correct answer is Choice C.

Question 2

Evolution is the cumulative effect of adaptations, but which adaptation gains ascendency over which is a point of interest. Predator-prey dynamics is certainly an important aspect. The relation between predator and prey is a bit like an evolutionary arms race. As soon as one develops a weapon or a defence mechanism, the other is working on an adaptation that allows it to _____ that mechanism.

Which choice completes the text with the most logical and precise word or phrase?

A) augment
B) assist
C) adapt
D) circumvent

Explanation

Brain Work:

The text talks about how predator-prey dynamics influences evolution. The second sentence talks about the evolutionary reaction of prey to predator and vice versa. If predator develops a new adaptation, the prey tries to 'outsmart' it, and the same is the case with prey as well. Thus, the word required in the blank should have a sense of 'outsmarting'. We should verify the options with this awareness.

Specifics:

Choice A: the word 'augment' (with a sense of 'increasing') is not fit because, if a predator develops an adaptation, a prey is not likely to 'augment' it. Thus, this option is incorrect.

Choice B: the word 'assist' is not logical in the blank – the reason being same as the one for Choice A.

Choice C: the word 'adapt' is not logical, because the adaptation of a predator is not likely to be undertaken by the predator – the purposes of adaptations are different; the predator's is to kill and the prey's is to escape from the predator.

Choice D: the word 'circumvent' (with a sense of 'finding a way around') is logically fit in the blank.

Verdict:

Thus, the correct answer is Choice D.

Question 3

One human and animal behavior that has been observed for years, but is poorly understood, is yawning, which is clearly associated with sleepiness and boredom. However, almost _____, it is theorized that yawning is perhaps a reflex that your brain induces to wake you up or make you more alert. It has been observed that yawning is associated with release of some hormones that prune us for action.

Which choice completes the text with the most logical and precise word or phrase?

A) certainly
B) paradoxically
C) consciously
D) ridiculously

Explanation

Brain Work:

The text talks about a hypothesis about yawning. Generally, it is associated with sleepiness and boredom. The use of 'however' indicates that the reason for it is contrary to what is usually accepted. By understanding the context, we can infer that the word required in the blank should have a sense of 'unexpectedness'. We need to verify the options with this information in mind.

Specifics:

Choice A: while the use of 'certainly' is likely to make sense in the context, the use of 'perhaps' in the following clause makes this option incorrect. Thus, this option is incorrect.

Choice B: the word gives the sense required in the context and thus, this is the correct option.

Choice C: the word 'consciously' is not logical in the context, because this word cannot modify the very 'theorized'. Thus, this option is incorrect.

Choice D: the word 'ridiculous' is not fit in the context because the final sentence of the text gives an acceptable scientific reason for the theorizing.

Verdict:

Thus, the correct answer is Choice B.

Question 4

Marquis de Condorcet, a radical thinker for his time and lineage, argued in 1780 that the rights of men stem exclusively from the fact that they are sentient beings, capable of acquiring moral ideas and of reasoning upon them. Since women have the same qualities, he argued, they _____ also have the same rights; either no member of the human race has any true rights, or else they all have the same ones.

Which choice completes the text with the most logical and precise word or phrase?

    A) arguably
    B) necessarily
    C) prominently
    D) tentatively

Explanation

Brain Work:

The text declares that Marquis was a radical thinker for his age and, thus, he was likely to argue for equal right for women. He argued that, since women have the same capabilities as men, they 'must' have the same rights as men. Thus, the word required in the blank must have the sense of 'compulsion' implied by 'must'. We need to verify options in the light of this information.

Specifics:

Choice A: the word 'arguably' has a sense of 'being very possibly true, if not certainly true' and this word does indicate the compulsion required in the blank. Thus, this option is incorrect.

Choice B: the word 'necessarily' gives the required sense in the blank. Thus, this is the correct option.

Choice C: this option is incorrect because the word is inapt for the sense required.

Choice D: the word 'tentative', which has a sense of uncertainty is not logically fit in the context.

Verdict:

Thus, the correct answer is Choice B.

<u>Question 5</u>

Tamburlaine the Great is a play in two parts by Christopher Marlowe, and is loosely based on the life of the Central Asian emperor Timur. Written in 1587 or 1588, the play is _____ in Elizabethan public drama; it marks a turning away from the clumsy language and loose plotting of the earlier Tudor dramatists, and also marks a new interest in fresh and vivid language, memorable action and intellectual complexity.

Which choice completes the text with the most logical and precise word or phrase?

A) a benchmark
B) an achievement
C) a milestone
D) an exception

Explanation

Brain Work:

The first line introduces a play written by Marlowe and the second sentence comments on the play. The second sentence contains a semi-colon which is followed by a part that explains the concept present before the semicolon. Thus, we can infer that the book marks a great change in Elizabethan public drama. The correct answer should reflect this concept.

Specifics:

Choice A: the word 'benchmark' denotes a standard with which the others are compared. The second sentence does not contain a word or phrase that implies this 'standard' and thus, this option is incorrect.

Choice B: while the word 'achievement' is certainly acceptable in the blank, the part after the semicolon does not give any indication of achievement on the part of the playwright. Thus, this option is incorrect.

Choice C: this word gives the required sense hinted at by the part after the semicolon and thus, this is the correct option.

Choice D: if the part after semicolon had noted what the play is an exception for, this word would have been justified. In the absence of such information, this option is not fit for the blank.

Verdict:

Thus, the correct answer is Choice C.

Question 6

In his book *The Fourth Amendment: Original Understanding and Modern Policing,* Michael J.Z. Mannheimer gives some observations. Police are required to obey the law. While that seems obvious, courts have lost track of that requirement due to _____ the constitutional provisions: the Fourth and the Fourteenth Amendments, which govern police conduct.

Which choice completes the text with the most logical and precise word or phrase?

A) overlapping
B) upholding
C) resorting to
D) misinterpreting

Explanation

Brain Work:

By understanding the context and the use of 'while', we can infer that police are sometimes not obeying the law due to 'some action' of courts. We need to identify the option that hints at the misuse of the constitutional provisions governing police conduct. We should verify the options in the light of this information.

Specifics:

Choice A: by 'overlapping' the constitutional provisions governing police conduct, courts are likely to 'correct' modern policing, and this is not the sense intended in the text. Thus, this option is incorrect.

Choice B: by 'upholding' (which has one meaning of 'defending against') the provisions, courts are not likely to result in some violations of the provisions (as hinted at in the context). Thus, this word is not a logical fit in the blank.

Choice C: by 'resorting to' those provisions, courts are highly unlikely to result in unwanted police behavior. Thus, this option is not logically fit in the blank.

Choice D: when courts 'misinterpret' the constitutional provisions governing police conduct, it is possible that police might violate the said constitutional provisions. Thus, this word is logical in the blank.

Verdict:

Thus, the correct answer is Choice D.

In a meeting with legislators in September 1862, Otto Von Bismarck, Iron Chancellor who unified Germany, made a statement which would become _____: "The great questions of the day will not be decided by speeches and resolutions of majorities...but by blood and Iron." He later complained that his words were taken out of context and miscon-strued, but 'blood and iron' became a popular nickname for his policies.

Which choice completes the text with the most logical and precise word or phrase?

A) influential
B) notorious
C) proverbial
D) satirical

Explanation

Brain Work:

The text quotes Bismarck's statement in a legislators' meeting. Later, he complained that his words were taken out of context and were misconstrued (misunderstood). The whole context implies that his statement later gained bad reputation. We need to verify the options in the light of this understanding.

Specifics:

Choice A: the word 'influential' does not have the negative connotation that is required in the context. Thus, this option is incorrect.

Choice B: the word 'notorious' is best fit, from among the options and thus, is the correct option for this the question.

Choice C: the word 'proverbial' (which means 'byword' or 'commonly spoken of') is not logically fit in the blank.

Choice D: the word 'satirical', with an implication of satire, is not logical in the blank.

Verdict:

Thus, the correct answer is Choice B.

Question 8

The following text is from E. M. Forster's 1908 novel *A Room With A View*. Lucy Honeychurch, a Briton, was on tour to Italy and was in a hotel room.

> It so happened that Lucy [Honeychurch], who found daily life rather chaotic, entered a more solid world when she opened the piano. She was then no longer either deferential or patronizing; no longer either a rebel or a slave. The kingdom of music is not the kingdom of this world; it will accept those whom breeding and intellect and culture have alike rejected. The commonplace person begins to play, and shoots into the empyrean without effort, whilst we look up, marvelling how he has escaped us, and thinking how we could worship him and love him.

Which choice best states the main purpose of the text?

A) To describe the feeling of divinity brought upon by appreciation of great music
B) To depict the ethereal nature of the composition on the piano
C) To describe how passionate Lucy was about music, which is beyond human bias
D) To bring out how Lucy compares to another person with great musical skills

Explanation

Brain Work:

To answer this type, we need to understand the central concept of the given text. The first sentence says how Lucy feels when she opens the piano. The second sentence depicts how she goes above the narrower feelings of the physical world. Later, the author uses first person to comment on the divine feeling musical world offers to the musician. Basing on this information, we need to verify each option individually.

Specifics:

Choice A: this option does not mention the central character Lucy, who plays music on the piano. In fact, the text describes the pleasure of playing music, not of appreciation of divine music. Thus, this option is incorrect.

Choice B: this option focuses on the composition on the piano, but ignores the person (Lucy) who enjoys playing music. Thus, this option does not give the central idea of the text.

Choice C: this option captures the central idea of the text and thus, is the correct option.

Choice D: the text does not present any comparison and thus, this option is incorrect.

Verdict:

Thus, the correct answer is Choice C.

Question 9

Text 1

Many drugs tested as effective cancer treatment failed in one crucial aspect: they also damage healthy tissues, causing serious side effects. Recently researchers modified a once-promising chemotherapy that had been abandoned due to damage it causes in gut tissues into a compound with "on" and "off" switches. The "on" switch was designed to be triggered by enzymes found in tumors, but not normal tissues, covering the compound into an active cancer drug. The 'off' switch, of course, is the enzyme produced by normal tissues.

Text 2

Dr Barbara Slusher who led a study of a new drug DRP-104 on mice said that the drug is as good at eliminating tumour as the original drug. In addition to directly killing tumor cells, the new drug also had another, equally important, effect in human clinical trials: it boosted the ability of a type of immune cell to kill cancer cells, helping to prevent tumors from coming back. "To have a drug that [not only] kills cancer cells but [also] activates immune cells is unique," Dr Slusher commented.

Based on the text, what would the author of Text 1 most likely to say about the study results mentioned in Text 2?

A) Though the new drug supports the optimization the modification presents, it presents a limitation needing our attention.
B) The study results have brought out a new benefit of our current research, despite the fact that they argue against our primary observation.
C) Besides endorsing our current research results, the results offer an added bonus to our expected result.
D) The results of our research are at variance with the results of that study, though their objective is common.

Explanation

Brain Work:

To answer this type of question, we need to understand the gist of each text and also the connection between them, before we attempt to verify answers. The first text talks about a new modification of cancer drugs which have serious side effects. The second talks about how a modified drug is effective and also talks about the additional advantage of improving the immunity against that particular cancer. We need to work on the options with this understanding.

Specifics:

Choice A: the new drug does support the modification process mentioned in the first text, but it does not put forward any limitation of the process. Thus, this option is incorrect.

Choice B: the first part of the option does correctly mention the new benefit, but the second part makes the option wrong; the results of the study in the text 2 do not argue against the primary observation (of removing the side effects of cancer treatments).

Choice C: this option is correct because it correctly expresses the endorsement of the results mentioned in the first text and also correctly mentions the bonus (immunity mentioned).

Choice D: this option is incorrect because the results are not at variance with each other.

Verdict:

Thus, the correct answer is Choice C.

The following text is adapted from William Shakespeare's 1609 poem "Sonnet 30". The poem describes the poet who is in pensive mood.

When to the sessions of sweet silent thought
I summon up remembrance of things past,
I sigh the lack of many a thing I sought,
And with old woes new wail my dear time's waste
Then can I drown an eye, unused to flow,
For precious friends hid in death's dateless night'
And weep afresh love's long since cancelled woe,
And moan the expense of many a vanished sight:

What is the main idea of the text?

A) The poet reminisces about the past and wastes his present which is valuable.
B) The poet remembers the past sorrows and compares them with the present's.
C) The poet remembers the sorrowful past and feels sad for wasting that time.
D) The poet remembers the regrets of the past and feels pensive again.

Explanation

Brain work:

To answer this type of question, we need to understand the central idea of the text given. The poet is in a thoughtful mood, and remembers the past things. He feels sad for not achieving his aspirations, and regrets wasting the valuable time. Being unaccustomed to weeping, he now cries for his dead friends and lost lovers. He feels sad for the faded memories. These are the ideas that are present in the text. We need to verify options basing on this information.

Specifics:

Choice A: the idea present in the first part of the option is correct, but no part in the text hints at the idea that he is wasting his valuable present. Thus, this option is incorrect.

Choice B: while the poet does remember the past sorrow, the text does not suggest that he is comparing them to the present one.

Choice C: this option is incorrect because no line in the text implies that he feels sad for wasting that time.

Choice D: this option is correct because this option captures the essence of the lines.

Verdict:

Thus, the correct answer is Choice D.

Question 11

The following text is adapted from Herman Melville's 1851 novel *Moby-Dick*. The following is the first-person narration of Ishmael, a character seeking employment as a sailor on a whaling boat.

What of it, if some old hunks of a sea-captain order me get a broom and sweep down the decks? What does that indignity amount to, weighed, I mean, in the scales of the New Testament? Do you think archangel Gabriel thinks anything the less of me, because I promptly and respectfully obey that old hunks in that particular instance?

Who ain't a slave? Tell me that.

Well, then, however the old sea-captains may order me about, I have the satisfaction of knowing that it is all right; that everybody else is one way or other served in much the same way; and so the universal thump is passed round, and all hands should rub each other's shoulder-blades, and be content.

Based on the text, how does Ishmael mentally respond to the treatment he might receive in the potential employment?

A) He fights back the temptation to undertake the employment, given the possibility of ill-treatment.
B) He entertains a resigned attitude given the inevitability of ill-treatment in most walks of life.
C) He considers himself lucky to find employment as a sailor, despite the ill-treatment that is in store for him.
D) He becomes resigned towards the ill-treatment because of his deep religious beliefs he entertains.

Explanation

Brain work:

Given the nature of the question, it might be advisable to read and interpret the passage with the requirement of the question; as per the question, we might look for key concepts that indicate what his feelings would be about the treatment he might receive. In the first sentence, the narrator describes the ill-treatment he might be exposed to. Then he broaches up religious observation and raises a rhetorical question; who isn't a slave? Then he mentions the 'the satisfaction of knowing that it is all right'. this implies that he is not likely to take ill-treatment seriously. With this information in mind, we need to verify each option.

Specifics:

Choice A: the passage states that the narrator is likely to tolerate the ill-treatment, while this option states about 'not taking up the employment. Thus, this option is incorrect.

Choice B: this option correctly describes what he is going to do; he has decided to tolerate the ill-treatment and also states that 'the universal thump is everywhere', implying that he might receive the same kind of treatment anywhere else. Thus, this is the correct option.

Choice C: this option talks about being lucky to find employment, and this concept is not given anywhere in the passage. Thus, we cannot infer this as his reaction. Thus, this option is incorrect.

Choice D: while this option correctly mentions the possible resignation, we cannot attribute this to the religious belief – note that no part of the text hints at this connection.

Verdict:

Thus, the correct answer is Choice B.

Question 12

The adventures of Ferdinand, Count Fathom is a 1753 novel by Tobias Smollett. Sir Walter Scott commented that the novel paints a "complete picture of human depravity (moral corruption)": _____

Which quotation (adapted for access to modern readers) from the book most effectively illustrates Scott's comment?

A) "Having thus inflamed her (Teresa's) love of pleasure, he hinted his design upon the young lady's (Teresa's employer's) fortune and promised Teresa that could he once make himself legal possessor of Mademoiselle, his dear Teresa should reap the happy fruits of his affluence."

B) "It was impossible for her (Teresa's employer) to overlook such studied emotions; she in a jocose manner taxed him with having lost his heart, rallied the excess of his passion, and in a merry strain undertook to be an advocate for his love."

C) "It would have been impossible for the mother of our adventurer, such as she hath been described, to sit quietly in her tent, which such an heroic scene was acting."

D) "Meanwhile, Ferdinand improved apace in the accomplishments of infancy; his beauty was conspicuous, and his vigour so uncommon, that he was with justice, likened unto Hercules in the cradle."

Explanation

Brain work:

The question actually requires us to identify a sentence that substantiates Scott's comment that the novel shows human depravity. We need to identify a sentence that shows depravity in some way. We need to interpret each option carefully because we need to identify evidence to support Scott's statement.

Specifics:

Choice A: this quotation describes his design (scheme or plot) and his cunning manipulation of Teresa so that she could help him to become legal heir of the affluence. These are indication of his wickedness and cunning to steal the inherited riches. This substantiates Scott's statement and thus, is the correct option.

Choice B: this option expresses how Teresa's employer falls in love with the protagonist. This does not illustrate the depravity and thus, is not the answer.

Choice C: this quotation describes a mother's love and thus, is not indication of the depravity we need to substantiate.

Choice D: this option describes infancy, which is not likely to be a proof for depravity. Thus, this option is not correct.

Verdict:

Thus, the correct answer is Choice A.

Scores given for two different scorers basing on different parameters
and the correlation between the scores

Category	Scorer A (mean)	Scorer B (mean)	Correlation
Content	2.99	3.10	0.70
Organization	3.99	3.40	0.70
Coherence & cohesion	3.65	2.86	0.67
Vocabulary use	2.69	2.78	0.81
Grammar & usage	2.62	3.39	0.85

In research on evaluation, a set of analytical essays written in English were evaluated by two scorers: Scorer A (a Japanese scorer) and Scorer B (a native English-speaking scorer). The essays were given scores (on a range of 1 to 5) basing on five parameters: content, organization, coherence & cohesion, vocabulary use, grammar and usage. Basing on the observations, the researchers claim that the correlation between the two scorers is high when the parameter used is an objective one related to compliance to rules rather than a subjective one judging standards.

Which choice best describes data from the table that support the researcher' claim?

A) Scorer B gives a higher mean score than Scorer A when the parameter is Content.

B) The Organization mean score of Scorer A is higher than his Content mean score.

C) The correlations between Scorer A and Scorer B are the same for two different parameters: Content and Organization.

D) The correlation between Scorer A and Scorer B is higher in Grammar & usage than it is in Content.

Brain Work:

The last sentence of the text gives information for which support is to be found from the data. The correlation between the two scorers is higher when the parameter evaluated is based on compliance of rules than when the parameter evaluated is related to subjective judging. We need to verify each option basing on this.

Specifics:

Choice A: this information compares mean scores given by two scores for a specific parameter; it does not compare correlation. Thus, this data is not relevant to the researchers' claim and thus, this option is not correct.

Choice B: this option too is incorrect because the correlation is not compared.

Choice C: this option is incorrect because the correlations are same, not higher or lower than the other, as is required by the context.

Choice D: this option is correct because evaluation of Grammar & usage is related to compliance of rules and evaluation of content is a subjective one and the correlation between the two scorers in relation to the former is higher than that in relation to the latter, supporting the claim.

Verdict:

Thus, the correct answer is Choice D.

Question 14

Christopher Hsee, a professor of Behavioral Science and Marketing, Booth School of Business argues that value perception is a fundamental aspect that makes marketing success, because value, a sense of worth, usefulness, or importance attached to something in this context, decides a purchase decision. People do not know what they want if you ask them. They decide what they want after reviewing context and comparative evaluation is easier. Psychologists have claimed to have found evidence for Christopher's claim in a recent study in which same volume of ice-cream of same quality was sold.

Which finding from the study, if true, would most strongly support Christopher's explanation for marketing success?

A) An ice cream vender selling ice cream at a larger shop sells as much ice cream as one selling at a smaller shop.

B) A vender selling the ice cream in smaller tubs sold more ice cream than the same ice cream in larger tubs.

C) A downtown ice cream vendor sells more ice cream than the one selling it in sub-urbs.

D) An ice cream brand that is more advertised during summer than it is during winter.

Explanation

Brain Work

Christopher explained success in marketing by invoking the idea of value perception. In this connection, he also introduced the process of comparative evaluation. We need to identify a piece of evidence that supports this explanation.

Specifics:

Choice A: this option does have the concept of comparison (larger v/s smaller shops), but both sell the same quantify of ice cream, and this argues against the explanation given. Thus, this option is incorrect.

Choice B: this option implies that the same quantity of ice cream in smaller cup appears to have more value than does ice cream in a larger cup and the higher sales of the former gives proof for the explanation given. Thus, this is the correct option.

Choice C: this option is not relevant because the sales were because of potentially higher demand present in busy areas than in sub-urbs.

Choice D: this option is incorrect because this option does not talk about the sales.

Verdict:

Thus, the correct answer is Choice B.

Question 15

The table below compares GDP per capita (in US dollars) indicating the economic growth, at the technological frontier, of four countries: The United States of America, the United Kingdom, Japan and China between 1960 and 2000.

Name of the country	1960	1970	1980	1990	2000
America	18,175	23,691	29,949	36,982	45,886
Britain	14,118	16,593	20,612	26,189	33,211
Japan	7,164	12,725	21,404	29,949	31,946
China	874	1,178	1,930	2,982	4,730

During the forty years under study, there was growth in per capita GDP (in US dollars) of the four countries which are compared. However, the per capita growth in GDP in countries near technological frontiers (America and Britain) is less pronounced than that in countries (Japan and China) that are far away from the technological frontier. This growth rate difference is most clearly seen by comparing _____

Which choice most effectively uses data from the table to complete the statement?

A) the growth in Japan between 1960 and 2000 and that in China between the same years.

B) the growth in China between 1960 and 2000 and that in America between the same years.

C) the growth in Britain between 1960 and 2000 and that in America between the same years.

D) the growth in America between 1990 and 2000 and that in Britain between the same years.

Explanation

Brain Work:

In the table, the first two countries were the ones near the technological frontier, while the last two are the countries were away from the technological frontier. The growth in countries away from technological frontier was higher than that in countries near the frontier. We need to identify the evidence from the data in support of the claim. We need to verify options in the light of this information.

Specifics:

Choice A: this comparison is between two countries that were far away from the technological frontier and thus, this is not relevant to the claim to be supported.

Choice B: this comparison shows an eight-fold growth in a country far away from the technological frontier and a three-and-a-half-fold growth (approximately) in a country near the technological frontier. This shows the more pronounced growth as stated in the text. Thus, this is the correct option.

Choice C: this comparison is between two countries that are near the technological frontier and thus, this option is not relevant to the comparison.

Choice D: this comparison, which is between countries near the technological frontier, is not relevant.

Verdict:

Thus, the correct answer is Choice B.

Question 16

A software company has recently claimed that it has created an AI-software that undertakes creating writing as effectively as a highly creative human can. To make the writing thus created by the software 'natural', the scientists created the database of ten thousand human-created samples of fiction, which the software uses to model its output after. While the supporters of the software argue that creating a best seller soon requires knowledge of just some computer commands to be used by the software, critics argue that the software will never be able to replace creative writers.

Which of the following, if true, would most directly support the critics' argument?

A) The development of the software has required a lot of resources, and consequently, the program is likely to be very costly to buy.
B) The software requires as input complex information that decides different parameters to be used in the production of a creative work.
C) Spontaneity in writing is required to decide the flow of plot and this feature cannot be programmed in a software.
D) Artificial intelligence, the basis for the software, is being used in many fields to minimize human error.

Explanation

Brain work:

Overall, the idea is that creative writing is undertaken by an AI-based software and it will need just a few commands to write a book. However, critics point out that the software will never be able to replace creative writers. We need to identify a factor that supports the critics' argument.

Specifics:

Choice A: while this option talks about the costly nature of the software, it is still possible that the software can replace creative writers. Thus, this option does not support the critic's argument.

Choice B: despite the fact given in the option, the software can still replace creative writers, and thus, this option is not correct.

Choice C: if this information is correct, the software cannot be programmed to have the spontaneity that is required for successful creative writing and thus, this option supports the critics' argument.

Choice D: incorrect because this option argues against the critics' argument.

Verdict:

Thus, the correct answer is Choice C.

Question 17

More than 5,000 exoplanets have been discovered since the first one was discovered in 1995. To qualify as potentially life-friendly, a planet must be relatively small (and therefore rocky) and orbit in the 'habitable zone' of its star, which is loosely defined as a location where water can exist in liquid form on a world's surface. None of the exoplanets discovered till now hardly qualify for these conditions. However, this 'life-friendly' is just earth-like life-friendly, and these exoplanets thus

_____

Which choice most logically completes the text?

    A) may contain life in a form which is totally unfamiliar to us.
    B) might not contain earth-like life forms.
    C) are likely to be planets that are in habitable zones.
    D) are likely to contain earth-life at least with some probability.

Explanation

Brain work:

The sentence with the blank contains 'thus', implying that we need to find a conclusion that can be logically drawn about the exoplanets mentioned in the text. The correct answer should be supported by the information given in the first three sentences of the text.

Specifics:

Choice A: from the second sentence and the third sentence, we understand that any of these exoplanets are not 'life-friendly'. But the first part of the last sentence states the qualification that this 'life-friendly' is just earth-like life friendly, implying that the exoplanets may be habitable for life forms that are unlike earth's life. Thus, this option is correct.

Choice B: this option would have been the correct option if the last sentence had not had the information (that 'this 'life-friendly' is just earth-like life-friendly') in the first clause of the final sentence.

Choice C: the passage gives information about what habitable zone is, but it does not give any information to suggest that the exoplanets discovered are not in habitable zone.

Choice D: this option is incorrect because the information in the second sentence argues against this.

Verdict:

Thus, the correct answer is Choice A.

Question 18

Severe mental disorders, which are common, differ from severe physical disorders caused by mutations in a single gene, which appear very infrequently. For instance, achondroplastic dwarfism, the result of single gene mutation, does not occur in more than 4 in 100,000 people. However, mental disorders such as bipolar disorder and mental retardation affects around 1000 in 100,000 people. The fertility estimates of people with mental disorders are lower than norm. if it is the case that these disorders harmed reproductive success over evolutionary time, then these variant form of genes that predispose people to mental disorders should have been wiped out many millennia ago. The prevalence of such mental disorders suggests that _____

Which choice most logically completes the text?

A) in periods shorter than evolutionary time, severe mental disorders are contained effectively.

B) severe physical disorders due to genetic mutations are more detrimental to evolution than are severe mental disorders.

C) evolution sometimes presents results not expected, creating an evolutionary paradox.

D) severe mental disorders should have some beneficial effect on the evolutionary process.

Explanation

Brain work:

Overall, the text argues that severe mental disorders are expected to be removed over evolutionary time because the people with such disorders have lower reproductive success, but that has not happened. We need to understand what is suggested by such prevalence. We need to look at the options in the light of this information.

Specifics:

Choice A: when severe mental disorders are not controlled even in longer time span of evolutionary time, we cannot logically infer that they can be contained in shorter periods. Thus, this option is incorrect.

Choice B: basing on the prevalence of severe mental disorders, we cannot infer that some physical disorders are more detrimental than physical disorders caused by genetic mutation; in fact, severe mental disorder are more detrimental to evolution than severe physical disorders due to genetic mutations.

Choice C: correct because if something expected does not happen, it results in a paradox. Thus, this option is correct.

Choice D: incorrect because the beneficial effect of mental disorders cannot be inferred from the information; as common sense dictates, severe mental disorder are actually harmful for evolution. Thus, this option is incorrect.

Verdict:

Thus, the correct answer is Choice C.

Question 19

In Don Paterson's most recent collection, *The Arctic,* the poet is doing what he has always done best: these poems are formally adept, sharp, philosophical, funny. What is really exciting, however, is the that venturing into a new ground altogether – somewhere darker, less enlightened, harder to escape through verse – _____ this collection fresh and inviting.

Which choice completes the text so that it conforms to the conventions of Standard English?

A) make
B) are making
C) makes

D) have made

Explanation

Brain work:

The subject of the sentence in which the blank appears is 'venturing into a new ground' and this sentence needs a complete verb to make it grammatically correct. The information between hyphens is additional and we can ignore it to understand that a singular verb is needed to agree with the singular subject ("venturing into a new ground altogether").

Specifics:

Choice A: the plural verb 'make' does not agree with the singular subject and thus, this option is incorrect.

Choice B: the plural verb 'are making' does not agree with the singular subject and thus, this option too is incorrect.

Choice C: this option provides the needed singular verb and thus, is correct.

Choice D: incorrect because the plural verb 'have made' does not agree with the subject.

Verdict:

Thus, the correct answer is option C.

Question 20

The global prevalence of anxiety and depression soaring by as much as 25% during the first year of Covid19 pandemic, the lockdown splintered people's mental _____ sign of caution for healthcare providers and governments to track mental health issues with vigilance.

Which choice completes the text so that it conforms to the conventions of Standard English?

A) health, which is a
B) health. A
C) health; a
D) health, a

Brain Work:

By looking at the options, we understand that either punctuation or modification is being tested in the question. We need to verify each option in the light of this information.

Specifics:

Choice A: The use of which in this context implies that people's mental health is a sign of caution; logically speaking, it is the absence of mental health that is a sign of caution. Thus, this option is not logical in the context and thus, is incorrect.

Choice B: by using a period, the option indicates the presence of a new sentence. But the part present after the period is a sentence fragment, and this makes this option incorrect; note that a fragment is not acceptable in Standard English.

Choice C: after the semicolon, there is a sentence fragment, which is not acceptable in Standard English. Thus, this option is incorrect.

Choice D: this option presents punctuation and structure that conforms to the conventions of Standard English. Thus, this option is correct.

Verdict:

Thus, the correct answer is Choice D.

<u>Question 21</u>

In his book *The Journeys of Trees*, Zach St. George explores an agonizingly slow migration of forests. A forest sends seeds just beyond its footprint in every direction, but the seeds that go to the north – assuming the north is the more hospitable direction – thrive a little more than the ones that fall to the south, _____ in the long run a slow, but steady forest migration, which unfortunately cannot keep pace with climate change.

Which choice completes the text so that it conforms to the conventions of Standard English?

    A) causes
    B) to cause
    C) caused
    D) causing

Explanation

Brain Work:

The long construction in the second sentence has two main clauses connected by the conjunction 'but'. Ignoring the additional information present between the two hyphens, we understand that the subject of the second main clause is 'the seeds'. We should look at the options with this understanding.

Specifics:

Choice A: the use of the verb 'causes' do not agree with the plural subject 'seeds' and besides that we need a conjunction to connect the two main clauses. This conjunction is absent, resulting in a comma splice error.

Choice B: the use of to infinitive (to cause), which generally expresses the purpose, is not fit in the context and thus, this option is incorrect.

Choice C: the use of 'caused', which is in past, is not correct to express a current observation and also the construction results in comma splice error. Thus, this option is incorrect.

Choice D: the use of participle gives the required sense of 'natural result' of the action mentioned in the main clause. Thus, this construction is correct.

Verdict:

Thus, the correct answer is Choice D.

Question 22

The Bluest Eye (1970) is Toni Morrison's novel that depicts the story of Pecola Breedlove, a young African-American marginalized by her community and the larger society. A powerful interrogation of   to an idea of beauty, the book asks vital questions about race, class and gender and remains one of Morrison's most unforgettable works.

Which choice completes the text so that it conforms to the conventions of Standard English?

    A) what does it mean to conform,
    B) what it means to conform
    C) what conformity means: as
    D) what does it mean to conform?

Explanation

Brain Work:

The first sentence introduces Toni Morrison's novel and the second sentence comments on that book. By studying the structure, we understand that the phrase 'A power … of beauty' is a describing phrase (modifier phrase) that describes the book. We need to look at the

165

options in the context of the whole sentence and select the correct answer accordingly.

Specifics:

Choice A: the interrogative structure (what does…) requires a question mark at the end of the phrase. As such question mark is absent after the phrase or the clause, use of this form is incorrect. thus, this option is incorrect.

Choice B: in the absence of the question mark, the assertive form ('what it means…beauty') fits in the context grammatically. Thus, this option is incorrect.

Choice C: while the assertive form (what conformity means) is aptly used, the use of colon in the middle of the phrase makes this option incorrect.

Choice D: while this interrogative sentence is correct as such, it does not grammatically fit in the whole context and thus, this option is incorrect.

Verdict:

Thus, the correct answer is Choice B.

Question 23

The physiological response to exercise is dependent on the intensity, duration and frequency of the exercise as well as on the environmental conditions. During physical exercise, requirements for oxygen and substrate in skeletal muscle are increased, just as _____ the removal of metabolites and carbon dioxide.

Which choice completes the text so that it conforms to the conventions of Standard English?

A) are
B) is

C) do

D) will be

Explanation

Brain work:

The given text describes the physiological response of our bodies to exercise. The second sentence states that, during physical exercise, requirements for oxygen etc are increased. In the same way, the removal of metabolites and carbon dioxide also increases; the use 'just as' hints at this comparison. We need to note that the subject the last clause is 'the removal of metabolites and carbon dioxide'. We need to verify the options with this understanding.

Specifics:

Choice A: the plural verb 'are' does not agree with the singular subject 'removal' and thus, this option is incorrect.

Choice B: this option uses the correct singular verb 'is' that agrees with the singular subject 'removal'. Note that the main verb 'increased' is omitted in this construction because it can be understood from the context (study the following note for further information). Thus, this option is correct.

Choice C: the plural verb 'do' does not agree with the singular subject 'removal' and this option is incorrect.

Choice D: this option uses future, while simple present is needed to express general facts. Thus, this option is incorrect.

Verdict:

Thus, the correct answer is Choice B.

Fun fact:

Sometimes, we omit some words in our sentences when those omitted words can be understood without any ambiguity. This process is called ellipsis, which is frequently used. Look at the following example: I live in my world and you (live) in yours. Even though the verb 'live' is not used in the second clause, it can be understood from the context.

Question 24

On October 29, 1969, the UCLA professor Leonard Kleinrock and his student Charley Kline electronically sent Stanford University researcher Bill Duval the first message "lo", because the complete intended message "login" could not be sent because of system crash after entering the letter _____ subsequent improvements, roughly 450.4 billion emails, which contain data equal to information in almost a trillion books, were sent and received each day in 2022.

Which choice completes the text so that it conforms to the conventions of Standard English?

A) "o", after
B) "o". After
C) "o"; after
D) "o": after

Explanation

Brain work:

The first sentence talks about the first message sent electronically. The message was partially sent because of the system crash after entering the letter "o". Now, we need to decide what clause is described by the modifier phrase 'after subsequent improvements'. This modifier phrase cannot logically describe the earlier phrase about system crash, but it can logically describe the following clause. We need to verify options with this information in mind.

Specific:

Choice A: if we use a comma as it is used in the option, two separate sentences are incorrectly connected by comma, resulting in comma splice. Thus, this option is incorrect.

Choice B: using a period, as in this option, resulting in two sentences that clearly express the ideas. The prepositional phrase after the blank correctly modifies the following clause, giving logical sense. Thus, this option is correct.

Choice C: using a semicolon is incorrect because the sentence after the punctuation mark is not an explanation of what goes before it. Thus, use of semicolon is incorrect and this option is wrong.

Choice D: using colon is also not correct in the context, because what goes after the colon is not an exemplification of what goes before it.

Verdict:

Thus, the correct answer is Choice B.

Question 25

Rates at which young forests remove carbon from the atmosphere vary by orders of magnitude across the world; tropical countries in Central Africa have the highest rates, while countries in Central Europe have the lowest. By harmonizing detailed carbon measurement collected at different locations and combining them with cutting edge machine learning tools, an advanced computer model can consider different variables and _____ a viable solution for environmental problems.

Which choice completes the text so that it conforms to the conventions of Standard English?

A) develop
B) develops
C) developing
D) developed

Explanation

Brain Work:

The first sentence describes differences in rates at which young forests remove carbon from atmosphere. The second sentence describes what an advanced computer model can do by using information. The verb in the blank should agree with the subject, should be in the correct tense as per the requirement of the context and should also be parallel with the correct verb form. We should verify the options basing on this information.

Specifics:

Choice A: the verb form 'develop' is parallel to another verb form 'consider' giving the sense that the advanced computer model can develop a viable solution for environmental problems. This gives the required and logical sense. Thus, this option is correct.

Choice B: while the singular verb 'develops' agrees in number with the singular subject 'computer model', the use of simple present is not apt here, because the second clause talks about the ability of the program, not about the general observation that requires simple present.

Choice C: use of the verb form 'developing' is not grammatically fit in the context. To make this possible, we should not use 'and' before the blank. Thus, this option is incorrect.

Choice D: the use of past is not logical in the context because the situation describes a present ability, not a past action. Thus, this option is incorrect.

Verdict:

Thus, the correct answer is Choice A.

170

Question 26

Responsible for nearly 25 deaths per terawatt-hour of electricity produced, _____ the deadliest power source.

Which choice completes the text so that it conforms to the conventions of Standard English?

A) 35% of electricity worldwide is generated by coal,
B) the generation of 35% of world electricity is by coal, which is
C) world electricity's share of 35% is generated by coal,
D) coal, which generates 35% of electricity worldwide, is

Explanation

Brain Work:

The initial modifier phrase ('Responsible for nearly ... produced') should modify the subject of the sentence. Otherwise, it will result in dangling modifier error. We need to look at the options in the light of this information.

Specifics:

Choice A: the subject provided by this option ('35% of electricity worldwide) is not logically modified by the initial modifier phrase. Thus, this option is incorrect.

Choice B: the grammatical subject ('the generation... electricity') is not logically modified by the initial modifier phrase. This results in dangling modifier error and thus, this option is incorrect.

Choice C: the subject given in the option too results in modifier error and thus, this option is not correct.

Choice D: this option is correct because the subject is logically modified by the modifier phrase.

Verdict:

Thus, the correct answer is Choice D.

<u>Question 27</u>

DNA of Neanderthals, human ancestors that became extinct millions of years ago, pose many technical challenges to develop their genome because with time DNA becomes chemically modified and after thousands of years it is massively contaminated with DNA from bacteria. In his seminal study, Swedish _____ made discoveries concerning genomes of extinct hominins, an endeavour lasting several decades and winning him Nobel Prize.

    A) geneticist, Svante Pääbo,
    B) geneticist Svante Pääbo,
    C) geneticist Svante Pääbo
    D) geneticist, Svante Pääbo

Explanation

Brain Work:

By looking at the option, we can guess that the testing point is punctuation. In a sentence, we use essential information without commas and non-essential information with commas on either side of it. By looking at the context, we understand that the proper noun 'Svante Pääbo' is essential information because without this information, the sentence does not give intended sense. We should verify the options with this awareness.

Specifics:

Choice A: this option uses commas on either side of 'Svante Pääbo', making it additional information. But, with this noun being an essential piece of information, use of commas is incorrect.

Choice B: this option uses a comma after the subject, separating the subject from the main verb. It is not conventionally acceptable to use a comma to separate the subject from the main verb (unless additional information is present in between). Thus, this option is incorrect.

Choice C: this option is correct because the proper noun and the title are properly used without commas.

Choice D: this option uses a comma unnecessarily between the title and the proper noun.

Verdict:

Thus, the correct answer is Choice C.

Question 28

An obvious difference between freshwater and seawater habitats is salt concentration. Freshwater fish maintain the physiological mechanisms that permit them to concentrate salts within their bodies in a salt-deficient environment; Marine fish, _____ excrete excess salts in an environment with high salt concentration.

Which choice completes the text with the most logical transition?

    A) consequently
    B) for example,
    C) on the other hand,
    D) by definition

Explanation

Brain Work:

The first sentence talks about the difference between seawater and freshwater. The second sentence contains two parts separated by a semicolon. The sentence talks about concentrating salts within bodies of freshwater fish and the last clause talks about marine fish's excreting excess salt from their bodies. These two concepts contrast with each other and thus, the transition phrase should depict this contrast. We should verify options with this information in mind.

Choice A: the use of 'consequently' hints at the cause-effect relation, and, as no such relation exists between the clauses, the word cannot be used in the blank. Thus, this option is incorrect.

Choice B: the use of 'for example' implies exemplification, which is not present in the context. Thus, this option is incorrect.

Choice C: the use of the phrase 'on the other hand' hints at the contradiction shown in the context. Thus, this is the correct option.

Choice D: the use of 'by definition' hints at a definition being given after the semicolon and no such instance is present in this context. Thus, this option is incorrect.

Verdict:

Thus, the correct answer is Choice C.

<u>Question 29</u>

Structural color was documented in the 17th century, in peacock feathers, but it is only since the invention of the electron microscope, in 1930s, that we have known how it works. Structural color is completely different from pigment color. Pigments are molecules that absorb light, except for the wavelengths corresponding to the visible color. _____ the intricate nanoscale architectures of structural color do not absorb light but reflect it into particular wavelengths resulting in vivid, often shimmering colors.

Which choice completes the text with the most logical transition?

   A) Accordingly,
   B) In contrast,
   C) Presumably,
   D) Similarly,

Explanation

Brain Work:

To understand the logical transition phrase, we need to understand the relative nature of the two concepts presented in the sentences that border on the transition phrase. The text discusses structural colors and pigment colors. In the sentence before the required transition phrase, the text talks about molecules (pigments) absorbing light. The sentence after the transition phrase talks states that structural colors do not absorb light, but reflect certain wavelengths. These two are opposing concepts: absorption of light and non-absorption of light. We need to look for a phrase that depicts this transition.

Specifics:

Choice A: the use of 'accordingly' implies that the fact or situation which is a result of something stated in the earlier sentence. No such relation exists between the concepts stated. Thus, this option is incorrect.

Choice B: the phrase 'in contrast' expresses the relation existing between the two concepts described. Thus, this is the correct option.

Choice C: the word 'presumably' implies a situation that we think is possible (in the light of information present earlier). This is not the case and thus, this option is incorrect.

Choice D: the use of 'similarly' is obviously incorrect, given the contrasting nature of the sentences.

Verdict:

Thus, the correct answer is Choice B.

Question 30

Sonam Wangchuk, a technologist, innovator and social and climate change activist, has a deep understanding of his region. The entire Himalayan ecology is under pressure and the people of Ladakh have started experiencing the manifestations of climate change. In the scenario, Sonam has radically different views about the potential solutions. He, _____, needs to be heard, for he is informed, credible and sincere and is speaking on the basis of his experience.

Which choice completes the text with the most logical transition?

A) in other words,
B) surprisingly,
C) however,
D) to summarize

Explanation

Brain work:

The text talks about Sonam, whose views are radically different. The next sentence says that he needs to be heard. Overall, the context implies that though his views are different, he needs to be heard. Thus, the transition phrase needed in the blank should show this contrast.

Specifics:

Choice A: the use of the phrase 'in other words' implies restatement of some concept. This is not the context and thus, this option is incorrect.

Choice B: the use of surprisingly indicates unexpected outcome and this implication is not present in the context. Thus, this option is incorrect.

Choice C: The transition word 'however' hints at the required contrast and thus, this is the best option.

Choice D: the phrase 'to summarize' is not logically fit here, for the following sentence does not summarize concepts given earlier.

Verdict:

Thus, the correct answer is Choice C.

Question 31

While researching a topic, a student has taken the following notes:

- Gestation in mammals is the time between conception and birth, during which the fetus is developing in the womb.
- The length of gestation varies from species to species and also the breeding seasons of these species are restricted.
- The horse, a spring breeder with 11 months' gestation, has its young the following spring.
- The sheep, a fall breeder with a five months' gestation, has its young the following spring.
- During spring, food is most abundant for the grazing animals.

The student wants to correlate the gestation with the season in which the birth takes place. Which choice most effectively uses relevant information from the notes to accomplish this goal?

A) The length of gestation is independent of the season in which birth takes place.

B) Gestation is adjusted so that birth coincides with the period when food is most abundant.

C) Both the size of the breeding animal and length of gestation coincide with the season in which birth takes place.

D) Gestation period is a variant of the animal breeding during certain seasons only.

Explanation

Brain Work:

To answer this type of question, we need to study the information given in the notes and evaluate each option in the light of that information.

the given notes comment on gestation periods, the season in which breeding happens, and the season in which birth takes place. It also comments on a particular season in which food is most abundant. We need to verify option in the light of this information.

Specifics:

Choice A: this statement is incorrect because the length of gestation does depend on the season in which birth takes place.

Choice B: this statement is correct because this generalizes using the information present in the last three sentences of the notes.

Choice C: this statement uses the size of the breeding animal, which is not relevant to the notes taken.

Choice D: this statement qualifies seasons in which breeding happens and this is not using the data given, because this information goes beyond the scope of information given.

Verdict:

Thus, the correct answer is Choice B.

Question 32

While researching a topic, a student has taken the following notes:

- Recent research helped understand the relationship between blood pressure and blood viscosity (a factor showing 'thickness of blood').
- The study observed 49 normal subjects and 49 patients with untreated hypertension (high blood pressure).
- Systolic viscosity (viscosity when heart contracts) was 10% higher in hypertensive patients than in people with normal blood pressure.
- Diastolic blood viscosity (viscosity when heart dilates) was 25% higher in hypertensive patients than in people normal blood pressure.

- Systolic blood pressure is always higher than diastolic blood pressure in all subjects.

The student wants to provide an explanation for high blood pressure by connecting it to blood viscosity. Which choice most effectively uses relevant information from the notes to accomplish this goal?

A) The systolic and diastolic viscosities of blood are higher in hypertensive people than they are in people with normal blood pressure.
B) Normal people have higher systolic blood pressure than their diastolic blood pressure.
C) Systolic blood pressure in hypertensive people is higher than their diastolic blood pressure.
D) For some people, the viscosity of blood is higher than that in some other people.

Explanation

Brain Work:

The text talks about blood viscosity, hypertension and their comparison in hypertensive and normal people. Overall, the student wants to state that higher viscosity is likely to be the reason for higher blood pressure. We need to identify information from data that shows the causal relation between hypertension and higher blood viscosity. We need to verify options in the light of this understanding.

Specifics:

Choice A: if higher viscosities (both systolic and diastolic) are higher in people with high blood pressure than in people with normal people, this implies that higher viscosity is the reason for higher blood pressure. This comparison from the data supports the causal connection to be established. Thus, this is the correct option.

Choice B: this comparison is related to normal people and thus, this is not relevant to the causal connection between blood viscosity and hypertension. Thus, this option is not correct.

Choice C: this comparison between two blood pressures is not related to viscosity and thus, this comparison is not relevant to the causal connection to be established. Thus, this option is not correct.

Choice D: the higher viscosity mentioned in this option is not related to blood pressure and thus, this comparison is not relevant to the student's thesis.

Verdict:

Thus, the correct answer is Choice A.

Question 33

While researching a topic, a student has taken the following notes:

- Era of Good Feelings was said to reflect the national mood of the United States between 1815 and 1825.
- Although it is considered coexistent with James Monroe's two terms (1817-1825), it really began in 1815 during the last years of James Madison's presidency.
- The good feelings started with U. S's enactment of protective tariff and the establishment of the second National Bank.
- With sectional conflicts in abeyance, nationalism seemed to pervade the national mood.
- But by 1820, a longer conflict, especially due to slavery issue, was in in the offing, imperceptibly though.
- The era proved to be a temporary lull in conflict, while new issues were emerging.

The student wants to emphasize the misconception the name 'Era of Good Feelings' is likely to create. Which choice most effectively uses relevant information from the notes to accomplish this goal?

A) The Era of Good Feelings is wrongly said to coexist with Monroe's terms, while in fact it started earlier.

B) The sectional conflicts that were in abeyance were not an indication of nationalism during Era of Good Feelings.

C) The conflicts before the Era of Good Feelings were not as divisive as those after that Era.

D) The name Era of Good Feelings is a misnomer since it actually hid hostilities that would evolve into major conflicts.

Explanation

Brain Work:

As per the requirement of the question, we need to identify an option that emphasizes the wrong impression the name Era of Good Feelings is likely to create. We should understand the concepts given in the notes and identify the correct option.

Specifics:

Choice A: while this option does give a wrong notion about the Era of Good Feelings, it is not the wrong notion created by the 'name' of the era. Thus, this is an incorrect option.

Choice B: while this statement gives a possible wrong idea, this wrong idea is not created by the name of Era. Thus, this option is incorrect.

Choice C: this option is incorrect because this is not information that can be inferred from the text.

Choice D: this option correctly brings out the wrong idea created by the 'name' of the era. Thus, this is the correct option.

Verdict:

Thus, the correct answer is Choice D.

A small request from the authors

If you find this book useful, your feedback encourages us and so don't forget to give feedback on Amazon.com or whatever website you have downloaded this book from.

If you want regular practice with new questions, consider visiting our website www.RRDigitalSAT.com, and register. You will enjoy the consistent journey by learning through our **SAT Question of the Day.**

MATH MODULE 1

Directions: The questions in this section address a number of important math skills. Use of a calculator is permitted for all questions.

What is 20% of 10% of 3500?

A) 70

B) 105

C) 630

D) 1050

Explanation

Brain/Paper Work:

'of' translates into multiplication.

So, the given expression can be understood as 20% times 10% times 3500.

Or, 20% [(10%) (3500)]

Now, x% of a value means $\frac{x}{100}$ times the value
('per cent' can be understood as 'per every hundred').
So, 10% of 3500 = $\frac{10}{100}$ (3500) = 350

Specifics:

Choice A: correct as per the explanation.

Choice B: incorrect because this is a result of incorrect calculation (this is 30% of 350, not the same as 20% of 10% of 3500).

Choice C: incorrect because this is a result of incorrect calculation (this is 20% of 90% of 3500, not the same as 20% of 10% of 3500).

Choice D: incorrect because this is a result of incorrect calculation (this is 30% of 3500, not the same as 20% of 10% of 3500).

Verdict:

Thus, the correct answer is Choice A.

The price, p, in dollars, of an item is calculated by the equation $p = 2(1.1n + 10)$, where n represents the number of years since the item goes on sale. Which equation has the same solution as the given equation?

A) $p = 2.2n + 10$

B) $\frac{p}{2} = 1.1n + 20$

C) $p = 2.2n + 20$

D) $\frac{p}{2} = 2.2n + 20$

Explanation

Brain/Paper Work:

This seemingly complex problem is, in fact, fairly simple. The question in its entirety may contain a lot of information, but ALWAYS focus on the **question stem** – what is being asked of you?

The question stem did not ask you to identify

- what the '2' on the right-hand side of the equation signifies
- what the '1.1' on the right-hand side of the equation signifies
- what the '10' on the right-hand side of the equation signifies

The question stem asked you to identify an <u>equivalent</u> of the given equation! That's it!

All you need to do is apply your skills in solving a linear equation – what would the different stages of your solving be? Cross-check at every stage whether your output matches with any of the answer choices.

Here, you will notice that Choice C matches with the very first stage of solving – expand the multiplication of the right-hand side of the equation.

Specifics:

Choice A: incorrect because this a result of incorrect calculation (this missed out on multiplying the '10' with the multiplicative factor '2').

Choice B: incorrect because this a result of incorrect calculation (this would result in multiplying the '10' twice with the multiplicative factor '2').

Choice C: correct as per the explanation.

Choice D: incorrect because this a result of incorrect calculation (this would result in multiplying the right-hand side with a multiplicative factor '4', not '2').

Verdict:

Thus, the correct answer is Choice C.

Question 3

In a certain class of n students, one-third of them use blue ink. Of these, one-fourth also use black ink. The number of students who use both blue ink and black ink is at least 3. Which inequality represents this situation?

A) $n \leq 36$

B) $n \geq 4$

C) $\frac{n^2}{12} \geq 3$

D) $n \geq 36$

Explanation

Brain/Paper Work:

Understand that

- *at least* or *minimum* means the same = <u>that value and any value more than</u> that value (same as $\geq$)
- *at most* or *maximum* means the same = <u>that value and any value less than</u> that value (same as $\leq$)

Number of students who use blue ink = $\frac{n}{3}$

Number of students who also use black ink = one-fourth of $\frac{n}{3} = \frac{1}{4}\left(\frac{n}{3}\right) = \frac{n}{12}$

Number of students who use both ≥ 3

$\frac{n}{12} \geq 3$

Specifics:

Choice A: incorrect because this is a result of incorrect conceptual application ('at least' mistaken as 'at most').

Choice B: incorrect because this is a result of incorrect conceptual application or calculation ($\frac{\frac{n}{4}}{\frac{1}{3}} \geq 3$ or $n \geq 4$).

Choice C: incorrect because this is a result of incorrect conceptual application or calculation ($\frac{n}{4}\left(\frac{n}{3}\right) \geq 3$).

Choice D: correct as per the explanation.

Verdict:

Thus, the correct answer is Choice D.

Question 4

The functions f and g are defined by $f(x) = x + 1$ and $g(x) = 2x^2 - 1$. For what value of x is $f(g(x)) = 32$?

A) 2

B) 4

C) 7

D) 9

Explanation

Brain/Paper Work:

> *Important tip:* Observe that, on the SAT, for questions that have numbers (any real number) in answer choices, the answer choices are arranged in ascending order (almost all the time).
>
> You can use that to your advantage!
>
> Here's how –
>
> Plug back a couple of answer choices in the given (or arrived at after simplifying) (in)equation/expression.
>
> Which two answer choices? Try the middle two – Choices B and C.
>
> Depending on what result you get after plugging in, you will be able to decide on the correct answer.

Let 's implement this learning in the given question.

Choose Choice C as the value to plug in.

When $x = 7$, $g(x) = 2(7^2) - 1 = 98 - 1 = 97$

So, $f(g(x)) = f(97) = 97 + 1 = 98$

But, as per the question $f(g(x))$ should be 32, not 98.

So, plugging in a value greater than Choice C, which is Choice D, would only result in a value greater than 98. Therefore, it is not wise to spend time checking Choice D.

Choose Choice B now; if the value after plugging in equals 32, then Choice B should be the correct answer. If the value after plugging in does not equal 32, then Choice A automatically will become the correct answer. You do not need to spend time calculating again.

Here, when $x = 4$, $g(x) = 2(4^2) - 1 = 32 - 1 = 31$

So, $f(g(x)) = f(31) = 31 + 1 = 32$

Specifics:

Choice A: incorrect because this is a result of incorrect calculation (for this value of x, $f(g(x))$ will not equal 32).

Choice B: correct as per the explanation.

Choice C: incorrect because this is a result of incorrect calculation (for this value of x, $f(g(x))$ will not equal 32).

Choice D: incorrect because this is a result of incorrect calculation (for this value of x, $f(g(x))$ will not equal 32).

Verdict:

Thus, the correct answer is Choice B.

$$p = n^2 - 1$$

If n is a number chosen at random from the set $\{2, 3, 5, 7, 11, 13, 15, 17, 19\}$, what is the probability that p is a prime?

A) $\frac{1}{9}$

B) $\frac{2}{9}$

C) $\frac{7}{9}$

D) $\frac{8}{9}$

Explanation

Brain/Paper Work:

Simply put,

$$Probability = \frac{what\ is\ required}{what\ is\ available}$$

What is available:

Since n can be any number from the set of 9 numbers, the total number of possible outcomes (what is available) = 9

What is required:

Since p should result as a prime number, n should be chosen such that $n^2 - 1$ is a prime number.

Make a quick observation that all the numbers in the set are odd numbers except for 2.

So, except for 2, n^2 will be odd for all other numbers.

So, $n^2 - 1$ will be even.

Hence, it is sufficient to check whether $n^2 - 1$ will be a primes number for $n = 2$.

Indeed, it will result in 3, a prime number.

So, for only **one** value of n will $p = n^2 - 1$ be a prime number.

$$Probability = \frac{1}{9}$$

Specifics:

Choice A: correct as per the explanation.

Choice B: incorrect because this is a result of incorrect conceptual application or calculation.

Choice C: incorrect because this is a result of incorrect conceptual application or calculation.

Choice D: incorrect because this is a result of incorrect conceptual application or calculation (this will be the probability of a number other than a prime).

Verdict:

Thus, the correct answer is Choice A.

Question 6

Machine *A* bakes bread twice as fast as machine *B*. Machine *B* bakes 25 loaves of bread in 10 minutes. If both machines bake bread at a constant rate, how many loaves of bread does machine *A* bake in 4 minutes?

Explanation

Brain/Paper Work:

Machine *B* bakes 25 loaves in 10 minutes.

Machine *A* bakes 25 loaves in 5 minutes (since it is twice as fast as *B*) or 5 loaves in every 1 minute.

So, in 4 minutes, machine *A* bakes = 5 x 4 = 20 loaves.

Answer:

Thus, the correct answer is 20.

Question 7

The function *f* is defined by the equation $f(x) = 3x - 8$. If $f(a + 3) = 10$, what is the value of *a*?

Explanation

Brain/Paper Work:

$f(a + 3) = 10$

$f(a + 3) = 3(a + 3) - 8 = 10$

Or, $3a + 9 - 8 = 10$

$3a = 9$

$a = 3$

Answer:

Thus, the correct answer is 3.

Question 8

During summer, the local amusement park sells tickets at discounted price for groups of students. For a group of n students, it sells tickets at d dollars for each ticket for the first 20 students, and offers a discount of p dollars for each ticket purchased after the first 20. Which equation represents the total cost of the tickets for n students, assuming $n > 20$?

A) $20d + (20 - n)(d - p)$

B) $20d + (n - 20)(d - p)$

C) $20d + p(n - 20)$

D) $20d + p(20 - n)$

Explanation

Brain/Paper Work:

Cost of tickets for the first 20 students $= 20d$

Number of students remaining $= n - 20$

Discounted ticket price $= d - p$

Cost of tickets for $(n - 20)$ students $= (n - 20)(d - p)$

Total cost of the tickets $= 20d + (n - 20)(d - p)$

Alternatively, plug in dummy numbers for n, d, p. Make sure you take numbers which are easy for calculations.

Say, $n = 30$, $d = 10$, $p = 5$

Cost of tickets for the first 20 students $= 20 \times 10 = 200$

Number of students remaining $= 30 - 20 = 10$

Discounted ticket price $= 10 - 5 = 5$

Cost of tickets for 10 students $= 10 \times 5 = 50$

Total cost of the tickets $= 200 + 50 = 250$

Choice A: incorrect because n must be greater than 20. Here, $20 - n$ will result in a negative number.

Verify for the remaining answer choices to check which answer choice gives 250 as the value.

Specifics:

Choice A: incorrect because this is a result of incorrect conceptual application (20 should be subtracted from n, not the other way around).

Choice B: correct as per the explanation.

Choice C: incorrect because this is a result of incorrect conceptual application or calculation (<u>discount value</u> is multiplied directly when <u>discounted value</u> should be multiplied).

Choice D: incorrect because this is a result of incorrect conceptual application (20 should be subtracted from n, not the other way around).

Verdict:

Thus, the correct answer is Choice B.

<u>Question 9</u>

Triangles ABC and XYZ are similar, where A and B correspond to X and Y respectively. Angle Y has a measure of 90^0. $XY = 12$ centimeters, $YZ = 16$ centimeters and $AB = 20$ centimeters. What is the value of $\sin A$?

A) $\frac{3}{5}$

B) $\frac{2}{3}$

C) $\frac{4}{5}$

D) $\frac{4}{3}$

Explanation

Brain/Paper work:

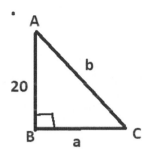 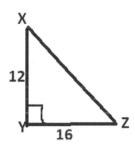

In Triangle XYZ,

XY = 12 = 3X4

YZ = 16 = 4X4

(3, 4, 5) form a Pythagorean triple. So, any multiple of a Pythagorean triple will also result in a Pythagorean triple.

Hence, XZ = 5X4 = 20.

It is given that XYZ and ABC are similar triangles. So, the corresponding sides must be in equal ratios.

AB/XY = BC/YZ = AC/XZ

20/12 = a/16 = b/20

20/12 = a/16 and 20/12 = b/20

Or, a = 80/3 and b = 100/3

Hence, SinA = BC/AC (opposite side to angle A / hypotenuse)

Hence Sin A = 4/5.

Specifics

Choice A: incorrect because this is a result of incorrect conceptualization. (This is cos A, not Sin A)

Choice B: incorrect because this is a result of incorrect conceptualization or calculation.

Choice C: correct as explained above.

Choice D: incorrect because this value is greater than 1 and sin of any angle takes a maximum value of 1.

Verdict

Thus, the correct option is Option C.

Question 10

$$x = 3k + y$$
$$y = x - 6$$

The system of equations is true for all values (x, y), and k is a constant. What is the value of k?

A) 0

B) 1

C) 2

D) 3

Explanation

Brain/Paper Work:

At the outset, it may seem like you are given 2 equations in 3 unknowns and that it would not be possible to solve the equations for k. But, observe that all the answer choices give numerals for the value of k. So, it should be possible to determine the value of k.

196

It is given that $y = x - 6$

Substitute this in the first equation in place of y,

$x = 3k + x - 6$

$k = 2$

Specifics:

Choice A: incorrect because for this value of k, the system of equations would become inconsistent.

Choice B: incorrect because for this value of k, the system of equations would become inconsistent.

Choice C: correct as per the explanation.

Choice D: incorrect because for this value of k, the system of equations would become inconsistent.

Verdict:

Thus, the correct answer is Choice C.

Question 11

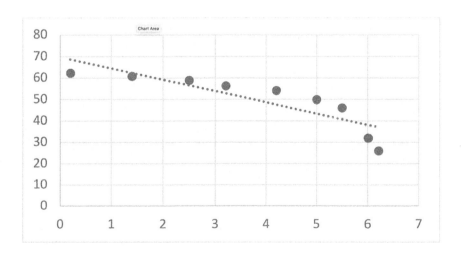

A line of best fit is shown for a given set of data points. Which of the following equations is the most appropriate linear model for the data points?

A) $y = -5.27x + 70$

B) $y = 5.27x + 70$

C) $y = -5.27x$

D) $y = -5.27x - 70$

Explanation

Brain/Paper Work:

Here, you should not spend time in trying to determine the exact equation of the trend line with the help of the x values and their corresponding y values.

A quick glance at the answer choices tells you that the numerals are the same across most of the answer choices. So, you should answer such a question through observations and inferences based on those observations.

Observe that the y values are decreasing as the x values are increasing. This shows a negative trend or a negative slope.

The standard slope-intercept form of a straight line equation is $y = mx + b$, where m is the slope and b is the length of the y-intercept.

Since the slope is negative in the graph, $m < 0$. This eliminates Choice B.

Also observe that the trend line cuts the positive y-axis (upon extending the line). So, $b \neq 0$ and $b > 0$. This eliminates Choices C and D.

Specifics:

Choice A: correct as per the explanation.

Choice B: incorrect because the slope here is positive; it should be negative.

Choice C: incorrect because in this equation, the length of the y-intercept is 0, which is incorrect as explained above.

Choice D: incorrect because in this equation, the y-intercept cuts the negative y-axis, which is incorrect as explained above.

Verdict:

Thus, the correct answer is Choice A.

Question 12

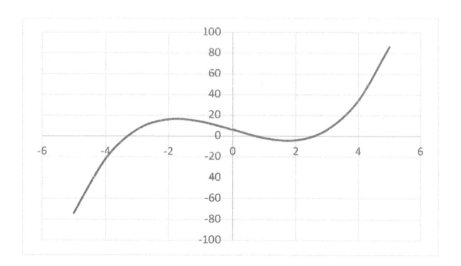

The graph of $y = f(x) = x^3 - 9x + 6$ is shown. For how many values of x docs $f(x) = 0$?

A) Zero

B) One

C) Two

D) Three

Explanation

Brain/Paper Work:

Here, you should not spend time in trying to determine the exact coordinates of the points that satisfy $f(x) = 0$.

A value x that satisfies $f(x) = 0$ will have the coordinate point $(x,0)$ which implies that it touches/crosses the x-axis at that point.

A quick glance at the graph tells you that the graph cuts through the x-axis three times or at three points.

So, you should answer such a question through observations and inferences based on those observations.

Specifics:

Choice A: incorrect as per the explanation.

Choice B: incorrect as per the explanation; in fact, the graph cuts the y-axis at one point.

Choice C: incorrect as per the explanation.

Choice D: correct as per the explanation.

Verdict:

Thus, the correct answer is Choice D.

Question 13

A math professor intends to convert a raw score x on a test into a new scaled score y by using a simple linear function $y = mx + c$.

According to this function, a student who gets a raw score of 90 receives a scaled score of 100. But, a student who gets a raw score of 65 receives a scaled score of 85. What is the value of m?

Explanation

Brain/Paper Work:

In the first case, $100 = 90m + c$

In the second case, $85 = 65m + c$

Subtract the second equation from the first,

$15 = 25m$

$m = \dfrac{3}{5}$

Answer:

Thus, the correct answer is $\dfrac{3}{5}$.

Question 14

x	2	3
y	-1	a

If the relation between x and y can be best represented by $y = x^2 - kx + 1$, what is the value of a?

Explanation

Brain/Paper Work:

Since one solution set is given (2, -1), substitute the same in the equation

$-1 = 4 - 2k + 1$

Or, $k = 3$

So, the equation is $y = x^2 - 3x + 1$.

Substitute the second solution set (3, a) in the equation

$a = 9 - 9 + 1 = 1$

Answer:

Thus, the correct answer is 1.

Question 15

A group of students volunteered for a community cause. It was observed that for each hour that passed while completing a specific task, the time taken by each student to complete a similar task decreased by 10%. Phil took 2 hours to complete a task when he started initially. Which equation represents the amount of time H, in hours, that Phil will take to complete the task after n hours?

A) $H = 2(0.1)^n$

B) $H = n(0.1)^2$

C) $H = 2(0.9)^n$

D) $H = 2(0.1n)^2$

Explanation

Brain/Paper Work:

Here, the efficiency of the students is decreasing with increasing time. Or, a student takes more time to complete the similar task as the time passes by.

So, the relationship will be an exponential equation indicating decay. The generic form for exponential growth/decay is –

$y = a(1 \pm r)^n$; choose '+' for growth and '-' for decay

where, a is the initial value, r indicates the rate at which the growth or decay occurs and n indicates the number of time periods after which the growth/decay is to be determined.

Applying this to the question,

$H = 2(1 - 10\%)^n$

$H = 2(0.9)^n$

Specifics:

Choice A: incorrect because this directly takes 10% and does not discount the 10%.

Choice B: incorrect because of incorrect conceptual application.

Choice C: correct as per the explanation.

Choice D: incorrect because of incorrect conceptual application.

Verdict:

Thus, the correct answer is Choice C.

<u>Question 16</u>

Which expression is equivalent to $\dfrac{5x^2-13x-6}{x-3}$?

A) $5x - 2$

B) $x - 3$

C) $5(x - 3)$

D) $5x + 2$

Explanation

Brain/Paper Work:

A quick observation of the answer choices will tell you that the numerator of the given rational expression can be factorized because none of the answer choices is in a $\frac{p}{q}$ form.

To factorize $5x^2 - 13x - 6$:

Split $- 13$ into two parts such that the sum of the two parts equals $- 13$ and the product of the two parts equals the product of 5 and -6, which is -30.

$-13 = -15 + 2$

Here, $(-15) \times (2) = -30$, which is the same as $(5) \times (-6)$

So, $5x^2 - 13x - 6 = 5x^2 - 15x + 2x - 6$

$= 5x(x - 3) + 2(x - 3)$

$= (x - 3)(5x + 2)$

Hence, $\frac{5x^2-13x-6}{x-3} = \frac{(x-3)(5x+2)}{x-3} = (5x + 2)$

Specifics:

Choice A: incorrect because this is a result of incorrect factorization.

Choice B: incorrect because this is a result of incorrect factorization.

Choice C: incorrect because this is a result of incorrect factorization.

Choice D: correct as per the explanation.

Verdict:

Thus, the correct answer is Choice D.

Question 17

The cost of manufacturing a refrigerator consists of the average cost of plastic materials, p, and the average cost of electronics, e. The total cost of manufacturing a refrigerator is t, and the situation is represented by the equation $pn + em = t$. Which of the following is the best interpretation of m in this context?

A) The average number of plastic materials used for a refrigerator in the manufacturing

B) The average number of electronics used for a refrigerator in the manufacturing

C) The total number of plastic materials used in the manufacturing

D) The total number of electronics used in the manufacturing

Explanation

Brain/Paper Work:

It is given that the cost of manufacturing a refrigerator consists of the average cost of plastic materials, p, and the average cost of electronics, e.

Also, the equation $pn + em = t$ represents the total cost of manufacturing a refrigerator.

The total cost of plastics or electronics can be determined by multiplying the average cost of materials and the total number of materials used.

So, in pn, n indicates the total number of plastic materials

And, in em, m indicates the total number of electronics

Specifics:

Choice A: incorrect because the average cost of plastic materials is already given and hence, multiplying the average cost with the average number of materials will not result in the total cost.

Choice B: incorrect because the average cost of electronics is already given and hence, multiplying the average cost with the average number of materials will not result in the total cost.

Choice C: incorrect because this would be n, and not m.

Choice D: correct as per the explanation.

Verdict:

Thus, the correct answer is Choice D.

Question 18

No. of Units Leased	Rental Value (dollars)
75	800
70	1000
65	1200
60	1400
55	1600
50	1800
45	2000

The table shows the relationship between the rental values, y, of different condominiums and the number of units leased, x. Which equation most accurately represents this relationship?

A) $y - -40x + 3800$

B) $40x + y = -3800$

C) $y = 40x + 3800$

D) $40y = -x + 3800$

Explanation

Brain/Paper Work:

The best way to solve questions like these would be to use the answer choices. Plug in any one set of values for x and y in any of the equations in the answer choices and check which equation holds true. That should be your correct answer.

Let $x = 75$ and $y = 800$

Choose Choice (C)

$$y = 40x + 3800$$

Now, $40x + 3800 = 40(75) + 3800 = 6800 \neq 800$

So, Choice (C) is eliminated.

Similarly verify for the other answer choices.

Alternate method:

A quick observation of the values in the table for both the columns (and/or the answer choices) will tell you that the No. of Units Leased and the Rental Values are linearly related.

This is because there is a constant difference between any two consecutive No. of Units Leased values and same is the case with the Rental Values.

The equation must take the form $y = mx + b$

Consider two sets of values – (70, 1000) and (45, 2000)

Substituting these values in the equation $y = mx + b$,

$$1000 = 70m + b$$
$$2000 = 45m + b$$

Subtracting one equation from another,

$$-1000 = 25m$$

Or,

$$m = -40$$

Plugging the value of m back into $1000 = 70m + b$,

$$1000 = 70(-40) + b$$
$$b = 3800$$

So, the equation is $y = -40x + 3800$.

Specifics:

Choice A: correct as per the explanation.

Choice B: incorrect because this is a result of incorrect conceptualization or calculation.

Choice C: incorrect because this is a result of incorrect conceptualization or calculation.

Choice D: incorrect because this is a result of incorrect conceptualization or calculation.

Verdict:

Thus, the correct answer is Choice A.

Question 19

The circumference of circle C is 18π. The radius of circle D is $2k$, where k is the diameter of circle C. The area of circle D is how many times greater than the area of circle C?

A) 9

B) 15

C) 16

D) 1296

Explanation

Brain/Paper Work:

The circumference of a circle is given by the formula $2\pi r$, where r is the radius of the circle.

The area of a circle is given by the formula πr^2, where r is the radius of the circle.

For circle C,

$2\pi r = 18\pi$ or $r = 9$ or diameter $= 18 = k$

Radius of circle $D = 2k = 2(18) = 36$

Since the radius of circle D is 4 times the radius of circle C, the area of circle D will be 4^2 times (or 16 times) the area of circle C.

However, 16 is NOT the answer for the question stem, though you will find it in the answer options (Yes, the test knows how students make errors)!

The question stem asks you to determine

- the number of times the area of circle D is **greater than** the area of circle C, and NOT
- the number of times the area of circle D is with respect to the area of circle C.

Therefore, if the area of circle D is 16 times the area of circle C, it should be 15 times greater than the area of circle C.

Specifics:

Choice A: incorrect because this is only the radius of circle C.

Choice B: correct as per the explanation.

Choice C: incorrect because this is the trap as explained above.

Choice D: incorrect because this is the square of the radius of circle D; it does not relate it to circle C in any manner.

Verdict:

Thus, the correct answer is Choice B.

Question 20

Data Value (degrees Fahrenheit)	Frequency
85	4
88	7
90	3
94	6
97	7
101	2
104	2

The frequency table gives information about temperatures, in degrees Fahrenheit, recorded in a city during a 31-day period. What is the median temperature, in degrees Fahrenheit, of the data set?

Explanation

Brain/Paper Work:

Frequency refers to the number of times a data value occurs.

So, the table should be understood as --- 85 occurs 4 times, 88 occurs 7 times, and so on.

A useful observation to make here would be that the values in the Data Value column are arranged in an ascending order. This is an important observation because, to determine the median value, the data has to be arranged in either an ascending order or a descending order.

If the data values are not given in a specific order, then you need to reorganize the data to determine the median value.

Now, since the number of data values is 31, the median of these would be the middle-most data value, the 16th data value.

The first three data values (85, 88, 90) together would make up a frequency of 14 (4 + 7 + 3). Since the next data value (94) has 6 occurrences, the 16th data value will definitely lie in this group of data values.

So, the median temperature of the data set is 94.

The same may be verified in a reverse order, from the last three data values (104, 101, 97).

Answer:

Thus, the correct answer is 94.

Question 21

A circle in the xy-plane passes through the point (3, 1). The equation of the circle is $x^2 + y^2 - 6x + 8y - c = 0$, where c is a constant. What is the radius of the circle?

Explanation

Brain/Paper Work:

Equation of a circle in the xy-plane takes the standard form $(x - h)^2 + (y - k)^2 = r^2$, where (h, k) is the center of the circle and r is the radius of the circle.

Now, the task is to bring the given equation into the standard form.

$x^2 + y^2 - 6^x + 8y - c = 0$ can be written as

$(x - 3)^2 + (y + 4)^2 - 9 - 16 - c = 0$

Since the circle passes through the point (3, 1),

$(3 - 3)^2 + (1 + 4)^2 - 9 - 16 - c = 0$

$25 - 9 - 16 - c = 0$

$c = 0$

The equation of the circle is now

$(x - 3)^2 + (y + 4)^2 - 9 - 16 - 0 = 0$

$(x - 3)^2 + (y + 4)^2 = 25 = 5^2$

So, radius of the circle is 5.

Answer:

Thus, the correct answer is 5.

Question 22

The angle made by arc AB at the center of a circle is $\frac{3\pi}{4}$ radians. Arc BC makes an angle $\frac{7\pi}{12}$ radians at the center of the circle. What is the measure of the angle, in <u>degrees</u>, made by arc CA at the center of the circle?

A) 105

B) 120

C) 250

D) 270

Explanation

Brain/Paper Work:

Observe that A, B and C are three points on the circumference of the circle.

To convert radians into degrees, multiply the angle measure in radians by $\frac{180}{\pi}$.

Angle made by arc AB at the center of the circle is $\frac{3\pi}{4}$ radians = $\frac{3\pi}{4} \times \frac{180}{\pi}$ = 135 degrees

Angle made by arc BC at the center of the circle is $\frac{7\pi}{12}$ radians = $\frac{7\pi}{12} \times \frac{180}{\pi}$ = 105 degrees

So, angle, in degrees, made by arc CA at the center of the circle = 360 − (135 + 105) = 120.

Specifics:

Choice A: incorrect because this is the degree measure of arc BC.

Choice B: correct as per the explanation.

213

Choice C: incorrect because this is a result of incorrect conceptualization and calculation.

Choice D: incorrect because this is a result of incorrect conceptualization and calculation.

Verdict:

Thus, the correct answer is Choice B.

Question 23

The age of the Sun is approximately 4.603×10^9 years, and one year is approximately 3.2×10^7 seconds. Which of the following is closest to the age of the Sun, in seconds?

A) 7.80×10^{16}

B) 12×10^{16}

C) 1.47×10^{17}

D) 14.73×10^{63}

Explanation

Brain/Paper Work:

The age of the Sun, in years, is given.

This value should be converted into seconds using the given multiplicative factor of 3.2×10^7 seconds.

When the whole number components of the two decimal numbers are taken, you get 4 and 3, the product of which is 12. So, the product of 4.6 and 3.2 must definitely be more than 12.

Also, when 10^9 and 10^7 are multiplied, the resultant will be $10^{(9+7)}$ or 10^{16}.

This logic will help you eliminate Choices A and B.

So, the closest value of the product should be 14.7 x 10^{16} or 1.47 x 10^{17}.

Specifics:

Choice A: incorrect because this is a result of incorrect calculation (4.603 and 3.2 are added instead of being multiplied).

Choice B: incorrect because this is value is lesser than the result.

Choice C: correct as per the explanation.

Choice D: incorrect because this is a result of incorrect calculation (the exponents are multiplied instead of being added).

Verdict:

Thus, the correct answer is Choice C.

Question 24

The graph of line m is the result of shifting the graph of line l 4 units right and 2 units up in the xy-plane. Line l is represented by the equation $3x - 2y + 6 = 0$. What is the y-intercept of line m?

A) (0, -4)

B) (0, -2)

C) (0, -1)

D) (0, 1)

Explanation

Brain/Paper Work:

$3x - 2y + 6 = 0$ can be re-written in the standard slope-intercept form ($y = mx + b$) as

$2y = 3x + 6$

Or, $y = \frac{3}{2}x + 3$

So, the slope $= \frac{3}{2}$ and the y-intercept is (0, 3).

Now, when the graph is shifted/translated, the positioning of the graph changes.

When the graph is shifted 4 units right, x becomes $(x - 4)$.

When the graph is shifted 2 units up, y becomes $(y + 2)$.

So, in effect, line m is

$$y = [\frac{3}{2}(x - 4) + 3] + 2$$

$$y = \frac{3}{2}x - 6 + 3 + 2$$

$$y = \frac{3}{2}x - 1$$

So, the y-intercept is (0, -1).

Specifics:

Choice A: incorrect because this is a result of incorrect conceptual application or calculation.

Choice B: incorrect because this is a result of incorrect conceptual application or calculation.

Choice C: correct as per the explanation.

Choice D: incorrect because this is a result of incorrect conceptual application or calculation.

Verdict:

Thus, the correct answer is Choice C.

Question 25

In the xy-plane, the graph of $x^2 + y^2 = 16$ intersects $y = x^2 + 2$ at how many points of intersection?

A) 0

B) 1

C) 2

D) 4

Explanation

Brain/Paper Work:

$x^2 + y^2 = 16$ is a circle with radius 4.

The standard form of a circle is

$(x - h)^2 + (y - k)^2 = r^2$, where (h, k) is the center of the circle and r is the radius of the circle.

$(x - 0)^2 + (y - 0)^2 = 4^2$

So, the center of the circle is $(0, 0)$ and radius is 4.

The standard form of a parabola is

$y = ax^2 + bx + c$, and it can be written as

$y = a(x - h)^2 + k$, where a, h and k are constants and vertex of the parabola being (h, k).

$y = x^2 + 2$ can be written as

$y = (x - 0)^2 + 2$

So, it has vertex at $(0, 2)$.

$y = x^2 + 2$ is a parabola opening upward.

217

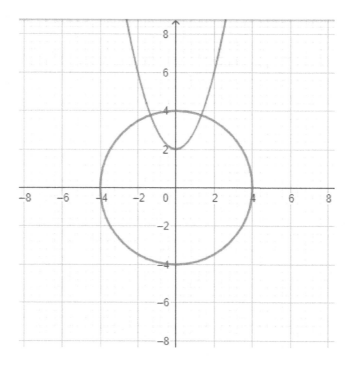

When you approximately draw the graphs of both the equations, you will notice that they intersect at exactly 2 points.

Specifics:

Choice A: incorrect because this is a result of incorrect conceptual application.

Choice B: incorrect because this is a result of incorrect conceptual application.

Choice C: correct as per the explanation.

Choice D: incorrect because this is a result of incorrect conceptual application.

Verdict:

Thus, the correct answer is Choice C.

Question 26

$$5x - 3y = 10$$
$$ax + by = 4$$

In the xy-plane, the graphs of the two equations intersect at 90 degrees at (5, 5). What is the value of b?

A) $\frac{3}{10}$

B) $\frac{1}{2}$

C) 3

D) 5

Explanation

Brain/Paper Work:

It is given that the 2 equations are perpendicular to each other.

So, the product of the slopes of the two straight lines $= -1$

Slope of $ax + by = c$ is $-\frac{a}{b}$.

So,

$$\frac{5}{3} \times \left(-\frac{a}{b}\right) = -1$$

$$5a = 3b$$

Also, $ax + by = 5$ passes through (5, 5) as that point is where both the lines intersect.

Substituting (5, 5) in $ax + by = 4$,

$$5a + 5b = 4$$

Substituting $5a = 3b$,

$$3b + 5b = 4$$

Or, $b = \frac{1}{2}$.

Specifics:

Choice A: incorrect because this is a result of incorrect calculation (this is the value of , not of).

Choice B: correct as per the explanation.

Choice C: incorrect because this is a result of incorrect conceptual application or calculation.

Choice D: incorrect because this is a result of incorrect conceptual application or calculation.

Verdict:

Thus, the correct answer is Choice B.

Question 27

The sides of a triangle are 9 centimeters, 12 centimeters and p centimeters. For what value of p, in centimeteres, will the triangle have the greatest area, in square centimeters?

Explanation

Brain/Paper Work:

One way to understand the area of a triangle is by the formula,

$$Area = \frac{1}{2}(product\ of\ the\ lengths\ of\ two\ sides)(sine\ of\ the\ angle\ between\ the\ two\ sides)$$

Now, for Area to be maximum, sine of the angle should be maximum.

It is known that $\sin(90^0) = 1$, the maximum value for sine.

So, when the triangle is right-angled between the sides 9 and 12, the area will be greatest.

So, $p = \sqrt{9^2 + 12^2}$, by Pythagorean theorem.

$p = 15$.

Food for thought: What would happen if you were to take the right angle between the sides with lengths 9 and p, with 12 as the length of the hypotenuse?

You should also note that you cannot take the right angle between the sides of lengths 12 and p because in that case, 9 becomes the length of the hypotenuse. This is illogical because the hypotenuse is the longest side in a right-angled triangle.

Answer:

Thus, the correct answer is 15.

A small request from the authors

If you find this book useful, your feedback encourages us and so don't forget to give feedback on Amazon.com or whatever website you have downloaded this book from.

If you want regular practice with new questions, consider visiting our website www.RRDigitalSAT.com, and register. You will enjoy the consistent journey by learning through our **SAT Question of the Day.**

MATH MODULE 2

Directions: The questions in this section address a number of important math skills. Use of a calculator is permitted for all questions.

Question 1

A laser printer prints y pages in t minutes. Which expression represents the amount of time, in hours, the printer takes to print $100y$ pages?

A) $\dfrac{t}{60}$

B) $\dfrac{t}{100}$

C) $\dfrac{3t}{5}$

D) $\dfrac{5t}{3}$

Explanation

Brain/Paper Work:

The printer prints y pages in t minutes.

The number of hours the printer takes to print $100y$ pages can be determined by setting up the proportion

$$\frac{W_1}{W_2} = \frac{T_1}{T_2}$$

where W_1 represents the number of pages printed in the first instance and T_1 represents the amount of time taken to print W_1 pages.

$$\frac{y}{100y} = \frac{\frac{t}{60}}{T_2}$$

t minutes needs to be converted into hours. Hence, the division by 60.

$$T_2 = \frac{100t}{60} = \frac{5t}{3}$$

224

Specifics:

Choice A: incorrect because this is a result of incorrect conceptual application (this merely converts t minutes into hours).

Choice B: incorrect because this is a result of incorrect conceptual application or calculation.

Choice C: incorrect because this is a result of incorrect calculation.

Choice D: correct as per the explanation.

Verdict:

Thus, the correct answer is Choice D.

Question 2

Betty drives t hours at a constant speed of 60 miles per hour to cover a distance of s miles. Which equation models the distance s if she increases her speed by k miles per hour so she can cover the distance in n fewer hours?

A) $s = (60 + k)(t - n)$

B) $s = \dfrac{60+t}{t-n}$

C) $s = k(t - n) - 60$

D) $s = 60k\left(\dfrac{t}{n}\right)$

Explanation

Brain/Paper Work:

$$speed = \frac{distance}{time}$$

distance = speed x time

$s = 60t$

Increased speed $= 60 + k$

Decreased time $= t - n$

$s = (60 + k)(t - n)$

Specifics:

Choice A: correct as per the explanation.

Choice B: incorrect because this is a result of incorrect conceptual application or calculation (this incorrectly relates speed, time and distance).

Choice C: incorrect because this is a result of incorrect conceptual application or calculation.

Choice D: incorrect because this is a result of incorrect conceptual application or calculation (this incorrectly multiples k and divides n when there should be addition and subtraction).

Verdict:

Thus, the correct answer is Choice A.

Question 3

$$5x + y = 5$$
$$-cx + 2y = 10$$

In the system of equations, c is a constant and the given system of equations has a unique solution (x, y). Which of the following is true of c ?

A) $c = -10$

B) $c = 10$

C) $c \neq -10$

D) $c > 10$

Explanation

Brain/Paper Work:

It is given that the system of equations has a unique solution (x, y).

The equations

$$a_1 x + b_1 y = c_1$$
$$a_2 x + b_2 y = c_2$$

have a unique solution when

$$\frac{a_1}{a_2} \neq \frac{b_1}{b_2} \neq \frac{c_1}{c_2}$$

So,

$$\frac{5}{-c} \neq \frac{1}{2}$$
$$c \neq -10$$

Specifics:

Choice A: incorrect because this is a result of incorrect calculation (when $c = -10$, both the equations become the same equation, with the second equation being a 2 multiple of the first).

Choice B: incorrect because this is a result of incorrect conceptual application (this takes into account only one possible value for c).

Choice C: correct as per the explanation.

Choice D: incorrect because this is a result of incorrect conceptual application (this takes into account only values greater than 10 for c, when in fact, even values lesser than 10 are also possible for c).

Verdict:

Thus, the correct answer is Choice C.

A taxi cab covers a distance of s miles in t hours arriving 40 minutes earlier than the scheduled time. What should the speed of the cab, in miles per hour, be if it were to arrive on time?

A) $\dfrac{s}{t+40}$

B) $\dfrac{3s}{3t-2}$

C) $\dfrac{s}{3t-2}$

D) $\dfrac{3s}{3t+2}$

Explanation

Brain/Paper Work:

$$speed = \frac{distance}{time}$$

Since the cab is 40 minutes ahead of schedule, the correct duration of time for the cab to cover s miles should be

$$t + \frac{40}{60} \text{ hours}$$

So,

$$speed = \frac{s}{t+\frac{40}{60}} = \frac{3s}{3t+2} \text{ miles per hour}$$

Specifics:

Choice A: incorrect because this is a result of incorrect calculation ('minutes' must be converted into 'hours').

Choice B: incorrect because this is a result of incorrect conceptual application (this assumes that the cab was 40 minutes late, when it is actually 40 minutes in time).

Choice C: incorrect because this is a result of incorrect conceptual application or calculation.

Choice D: correct as per the explanation.

Verdict:

Thus, the correct answer is Choice D.

Question 5

The angles of a triangle are in the ratio 1:1:2 and the length of one of the shorter sides is 5 units. What is the length of the longest side of the triangle?

A) $2\sqrt{5}$

B) $5\sqrt{2}$

C) 10

D) $10\sqrt{2}$

Explanation

Brain/Paper Work:

When the angles are in the ratio 1:1:2, two angles are equal in measure.

So, the triangle is isosceles.

Let the three angles be $x°$, $x°$ and $2x°$

Sum of the angles = 180^0

$x + x + 2x = 180$

$x = 45^0$

So, the angles are 45^0, 45^0 and 90^0.

Now, the triangle is right-angled isosceles.

Since the shorter side is of length 5 units, the hypotenuse will be $5\sqrt{2}$, by Pythagorean theorem.

Specifics:

Choice A: incorrect because this is a result of incorrect conceptual application or calculation (this value is less than 5, which is not logical because this value must be greater than 5).

Choice B: correct as per the explanation.

Choice C: incorrect because this is a result of incorrect calculation.

Choice D: incorrect because this is a result of incorrect calculation.

Verdict:

Thus, the correct answer is Choice B.

Question 6

Three times the first of 3 consecutive even integers, when placed in an increasing order, is 2 more than twice the third. What is the second even integer?

A) 10

B) 12

C) 14

D) 16

Explanation

Brain/Paper Work:

Two ways to determine the correct answer for this question –

Method 1:

Use the answer choices and check which one will satisfy the given situation. When choosing answer options, make sure you use this tip –

> *Important tip:* Observe that, on the SAT, for questions that have numbers (any real number) in answer choices, the answer choices are arranged in ascending order (almost all the time).
>
> You can use that to your advantage!
>
> Here's how –
>
> Plug back a couple of answer choices in the given (or arrived at after simplifying) (in)equation/expression.
>
> Which two answer choices? Try the middle two – Choices B and C.
>
> Depending on what result you get after plugging in, you will be able to decide on the correct answer.

Method 2 (the conventional way):

Let the three consecutive even integers be $2n - 2, 2n, 2n + 2$

$3 (2n - 2) = 2 + 2 (2n + 2)$

$6n - 6 = 4n + 6$

$n = 6$

The second integer is $2n = 12$.

Specifics:

Choice A: incorrect because this is a result of incorrect calculation (this is the first even number).

Choice B: correct as per the explanation.

Choice C: incorrect because this is a result of incorrect calculation (this is the third even number).

Choice D: incorrect because this is a result of incorrect calculation.

Verdict:

Thus, the correct answer is Choice B.

Question 7

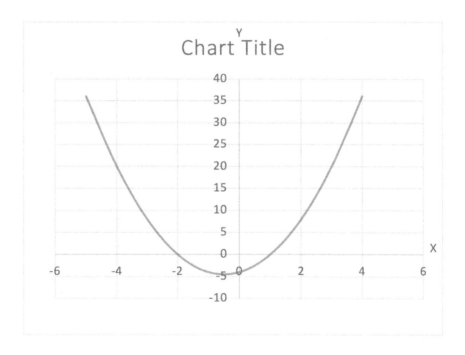

The y-intercept of the graph $y = 2x^2 + 2x - 4$ is $(0, y)$. What is the value of y ?

Explanation

Brain/Paper Work:

The y-intercept of the graph is $(0, f(0))$.

$f(0) = 2\,(0^2) + 2\,(0) - 4 = -4$

So, $y = -4$.

Alternatively, you may make a quick observation of the graph and notice that the graph passes through the x-axis at −2 and 1.

So, the x-intercepts are (−2, 0) and (1, 0).

Similarly, the graph passes through the y-axis at − 4.

So, the y-intercept is (0, −4).

Answer:

Thus, the correct answer is − 4.

Question 8

The function g is defined by $g(x) - 3x - 7$. What is the x-intercept of the graph of $y = g(x)$ in the xy-plane?

A) −7

B) $-\dfrac{7}{3}$

C) $-\dfrac{3}{7}$

D) $\dfrac{7}{3}$

Explanation

Brain/Paper Work:

The x-intercept of the graph in the xy-plane is the point on the graph where $y = 0$.

You are to determine the x-intercept of $y = g(-x)$ and NOT that of $g(x)$.

Given that $y = g(-x)$

So, $y = g(-x) = 3(-x) - 7$

$y + 7 = -3x$

$x = -\dfrac{1}{3}y - \dfrac{7}{3}$

When $y = 0$, $x = -\dfrac{7}{3}$

Specifics:

Choice A: incorrect because this is a result of incorrect conceptual application (this is the y-intercept of).

Choice B: correct as per the explanation.

Choice C: incorrect because this is a result of incorrect calculation.

Choice D: incorrect because this is a result of incorrect calculation.

Verdict:

Thus, the correct answer is Choice B.

Question 9

The function h is defined by $h(x) = |x - 2|$. Which of the following represents $i(x)$, where $i(x)$ is the result of shifting the graph of $h(x)$ 3 units up and 4 units right?

A) $i(x) = |x - 6|$

B) $i(x) = |x - 6| + 3$

C) $i(x) = |x + 2| + 3$

D) $i(x) = |x - 6| - 3$

Explanation

Brain/Paper Work:

For $y = f(x)$, when $f(x)$ is shifted up/down/right/left by k units, the resultant function $g(x)$ will be

1. $g(x) = f(x) + k$; $f(x)$ is shifted k units up
2. $g(x) = f(x) - k$; $f(x)$ is shifted k units down
3. $g(x) = f(x + k)$; $f(x)$ is shifted k units left
4. $g(x) = f(x - k)$; $f(x)$ is shifted k units right

Given $h(x) = |x - 2|$

When $h(x)$ is shifted 3 units up and 4 units right,

$$i(x) = |x - 2 - 4| + 3$$
$$i(x) = |x - 6| + 3$$

Specifics:

Choice A: incorrect because this is a result of incorrect calculation (the shift by 3 units up is not taken into consideration)

Choice B: correct as per the explanation.

Choice C: incorrect because this is a result of incorrect conceptual application or calculation (the shift by 4 units right is taken as 4 units left)

Choice D: incorrect because this is a result of incorrect conceptual application or calculation (the shift by 3 units up is taken as 3 units down).

Verdict:

Thus, the correct answer is Choice B.

$$16^x = 2$$
$$x^y = 64$$

Which ordered pair (x, y) is a solution to the given system of equations?

A) $(-\frac{1}{4}, -3)$

B) $(-\frac{1}{4}, 3)$

C) $(\frac{1}{4}, -3)$

D) $(\frac{1}{4}, 3)$

Explanation

Brain/Paper Work:

Method 1 (observation from the answer choices):

The value of x is a fraction, either $\frac{1}{4}$ or $-\frac{1}{4}$.

Since the base on the left hand side of the first equation can be expressed as a positive power of 2, which is the base on the right hand side, x value will be positive.

Similarly, the base on the left hand side of the second equation can be expressed as a negative power of 4 (since the base is a fraction), which is the base on the right hand side (4^3), y value will be negative.

Only Choice C suits.

Method 2 (conventional way):

$16^x = 2$

$(2^4)^x = 2$

$2^{4x} = 2^1$

$$x = \frac{1}{4}$$

Now, $x^y = 64$

$$(\frac{1}{4})^y = 4^3$$

$$4^{-y} = 4^3$$

$$y = -3$$

$$(x, y) = (\frac{1}{4}, -3)$$

Specifics:

Choice A: incorrect because this is a result of incorrect calculation.

Choice B: incorrect because this is a result of incorrect calculation.

Choice C: correct as per the explanation.

Choice D: incorrect because this is a result of incorrect calculation.

Verdict:

Thus, the correct answer is Choice C.

Question 11

Which expression is equivalent to $\frac{2x}{3x^2+6x} + \frac{x-1}{x+2}$, where $x \neq 0$?

A) $\frac{3x-1}{3(x+2)}$

B) $\frac{x-1}{x+2}$

C) $\frac{3x-1}{3x^2+7x+2}$

D) $\frac{6x-1}{3x^2+7x+2}$

237

Explanation

Brain/Paper Work:

$$\frac{2x}{3x^2 + 6x} + \frac{x-1}{x+2}$$

$$= \frac{2x}{3x(x+2)} + \frac{x-1}{x+2}$$

$$= \frac{2}{3(x+2)} + \frac{x-1}{x+2}$$

$$= \frac{2+3(x-1)}{3(x+2)}$$

$$= \frac{3x-1}{3(x+2)}$$

Specifics:

Choice A: correct as per the explanation.

Choice B: incorrect because this is a result of incorrect conceptual application or calculation.

Choice C: incorrect because this is a result of incorrect conceptual application or calculation.

Choice D: incorrect because this is a result of incorrect conceptual application or calculation.

Verdict:

Thus, the correct answer is Choice A.

Question 12

The function g is defined by $g(x) = 3x^2 - 5x + k$, where k is a constant. What is value of k when $g(1) = 0$?

A) -2

B) 0

C) 2

D) 1

Explanation

Brain/Paper Work:

It is given that $g(x) = 3x^2 - 5x + k$

$g(1) = 3(1)^2 - 5(1) + k = 0$

$k = 2$

Key Point to Note:

When g (*number*) = 0, it means that $(x - number)$ is a factor of $g(x)$. Or, the remainder when $g(x)$ is divided by $(x - number)$ is 0.

So, here, $x - 1$ is a factor of $3x^2 - 5x + 2$.

Similarly, when g (*number*) = n, it means that the remainder when $g(x)$ is divided by $(x - number)$ is n.

Specifics:

Choice A: incorrect because this is a result of incorrect calculation.

Choice B: incorrect because this is a result of incorrect calculation.

Choice C: correct as per the explanation.

Choice D: incorrect because this is a result of incorrect calculation.

Verdict:

Thus, the correct answer is Choice C.

Question 13

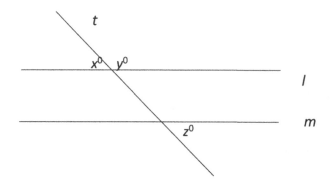

Note: Figure not drawn to scale.

In the figure shown, line t intersects parallel lines l and m. $x = 4p + 17$, $z = 9p - 13$, where p is a constant. What is the value of y?

Explanation

Brain/Paper Work:

Observe that x and z are equal to each other since they are exterior alternate angles with respect to the parallel lines l and m.

So, $4p + 17 = 9p - 13$

Or, $p = 6$

x should be equal to $4p + 17 = 41$.

x and y form a supplementary pair of angles.

So, $y = 180 - x = 180 - 41 = 139$.

Answer:

Thus, the correct answer is 139.

Question 14

In the list of data values

$$24, 18, 48, 30, x$$

the arithmetic mean, median and mode are all equal. What is the value of x ?

Explanation

Brain/Paper Work:

All the numeric values given in the data are unique numbers.

So, x must be the mode and must be equal to one of the remaining 4 values (since mode is defined as the most occurring data value in a given set of data values).

It is given that the Arithmetic Mean = Mode

So,

So, $\dfrac{24+18+48+30+x}{5} = x$

$120 + x = 5x$

$x = 30$

You would also notice that when the data values are arranged in ascending (or descending) order, the median would be 30.

Answer:

Thus, the correct answer is 30.

Question 15

The equation $C(n) = 100(1.15)^n$ gives the estimated cost of production of manufacturing a total of k items, where n is the number of years since the item is in production. Which of the following is the best interpretation of the number 15 in this context?

A) The percent increase in the estimated cost of production each year for k items

B) The increase in the absolute value of the estimated cost of production for each of the k items

C) The initial value of the estimated cost of production per each item

D) The increase in production over k items each year

Explanation

Brain/Paper Work:

The given exponential function $C(n) = 100(1.15)^n$

can be understood as

$C(n) = 100(1 + 0.15)^n$

Or, $C(n) = 100(1 + 15\%)^n$

This means that the initial cost of production is 100 (when $n = 0$) for a total of k items and that the cost increases by 15% every year.

Only Choice A explains this.

Specifics:

Choice A: correct as per the explanation.

Choice B: incorrect because this is a result of incorrect conceptual application (this is NOT increase in absolute value, but a percent increase).

Choice C: incorrect because this is a result of incorrect conceptual application (the initial cost of production for all the k items is 100).

Choice D: incorrect because this is a result of incorrect conceptual application.

Verdict:

Thus, the correct answer is Choice A.

$$f(x) = -2x^2 + 4x + 5$$

Which of the following is true of $f(x)$?

A) The minimum value of $f(x)$ is 5.

B) The minimum value of $f(x)$ is 7.

C) The maximum value of $f(x)$ is 5.

D) The maximum value of $f(x)$ is 7.

Explanation

Brain/Paper Work:

Any quadratic function can be expressed in the standard form $f(x) = a(x - h)^2 + k$, where a, h and k are constants.

When $a > 0$, $f(x)$ takes a minimum value of k because the graph opens up and it has a minimum point at the bottom of the graph.

When $a < 0$, $f(x)$ takes a maximum value of k because the graph opens down and it has a maximum point at the top of the graph.

$$f(x) = -2x^2 + 4x + 5$$

$$f(x) = -2(x - 1)^2 + 7$$

Here,

$a = -2$

$h = 1$

243

$k = 7$

Since $a < 0$, the graph takes a maximum value and it is 7.

Specifics:

Choice A: incorrect because this is a result of incorrect conceptual application (the graph does not take a minimum value).

Choice B: incorrect because this is a result of incorrect conceptual application (the graph does not take a minimum value).

Choice C: incorrect because this is a result of incorrect calculation (here, the constant term 5 is assumed to be the value, when it should be 7 as explained).

Choice D: correct as per the explanation.

Verdict:

Thus, the correct answer is Choice D.

Question 17

Every fortnight, Marie sets aside $100 from her earnings towards her savings. Which of the following accurately describes how the value of her savings changes as a function of time?

A) Linear and decreases with time

B) Exponential and decreases with time

C) Linear and increases with time

D) Exponential and increases with time

Explanation

Brain/Paper Work:

Since the amount of savings is

- increasing every fortnight, it is an increasing function

- constant ($100) every fortnight, it is a linear function.

So, the value of Marie's savings is Linear and Increasing.

Specifics:

Choice A: incorrect because this is a result of incorrect conceptual application.

Choice B: incorrect because this is a result of incorrect conceptual application.

Choice C: correct as per the explanation.

Choice D: incorrect because this is a result of incorrect conceptual application.

Verdict:

Thus, the correct answer is Choice C.

Question 18

On a standardized test, 40% of the 400 students from Glendale High School scored 90th percentile while 40% of the 500 students from Rockwel High School scored 90th percentile. The total number of students who score 90th percentile from both the schools is times the total number of students from both the schools. What is the value of ?

A) $\frac{2}{5}$

B) $\frac{4}{9}$

C) $\frac{5}{2}$

D) 360

Explanation

Brain/Paper Work:

Number of students from Gendale who scored 90th percentile = 40% of 400 = $\frac{40}{100} \times 400 = 160$

Number of students from Rockwel who scored 90th percentile = 40% of 500 = $\frac{40}{100} \times 500 = 200$

Total number of students who scored 90th percentile $= 160 + 200 = 360$

Total number of students from both the schools $= 400 + 500 = 900$

Given that

$$360 = p \times 900$$

Or,

$$p = \frac{2}{5}$$

Specifics:

Choice A: correct as per the explanation.

Choice B: incorrect because this is a result of incorrect calculation.

Choice C: incorrect because this is a result of incorrect conceptual application or calculation (this value equals $\frac{1}{p}$, and not p).

Choice D: incorrect because this is a result of incorrect calculation (this is the total number of students who scored 90th percentile).

Verdict:

Thus, the correct answer is Choice A.

Which of the following is equivalent to $\frac{32 \times \sqrt[3]{81} \times \sqrt{125}}{30}$?

A) $2^4 \times \sqrt[3]{3}$

B) $2^4 \times \sqrt[3]{3} \times \sqrt{5}$

C) $2^5 \times \sqrt[3]{3} \times \sqrt{5}$

D) $2^4 \times 3\sqrt[3]{3} \times 5\sqrt{5}$

Explanation

Brain/Paper Work:

$$\frac{32 \times \sqrt[3]{81} \times \sqrt{125}}{30} = \frac{2^5 \times \sqrt[3]{3^4} \times \sqrt{5^3}}{2 \times 3 \times 5} = \frac{2^4 \times \sqrt[3]{3^3 \times 3^1} \times \sqrt{5^2 \times 5^1}}{3 \times 5} = \frac{2^4 \times 3\sqrt[3]{3} \times 5\sqrt{5}}{3 \times 5}$$

$$= 2^4 \times \sqrt[3]{3} \times \sqrt{5}$$

Specifics:

Choice A: incorrect because this is a result of incorrect calculation.

Choice B: correct as per the explanation.

Choice C: incorrect because this is a result of incorrect calculation.

Choice D: incorrect because this is a result of incorrect calculation.

Verdict:

Thus, the correct answer is Choice B.

Question 20

A man purchases two different types of toys – the first type at $9 each and the second at $5 each. He spends a maximum of $115. What is the ratio of the number of toys of the second type to the first type so that a maximum number of toys of the first type are purchased at no additional cost? *(Express ratio as a fraction)*

Explanation

Brain/Paper Work:

The total expenditure = the total amount of money spent on the first type + the total amount of money spent on the second ≤ 115

Total amount spent on the first type = $9a$, where a is the number of toys of the first type purchased

Total amount spent on the second type = $5b$, where b is the number of toys of the second type purchased

So,

$9a + 5b \leq 115$

$a \leq \dfrac{115 - 5b}{9}$

To maximize a, you should minimize b.

Plug in the minimum value of $b = 1$

(both a and b are number of toys purchased and hence, they must be positive integers)

$a \leq \dfrac{115-5(1)}{9}$

or $a \leq \dfrac{110}{9}$

or $a \leq 12.22$

So, the maximum integer value of will be 12.

Answer:

Thus, the correct answer is $\frac{1}{12}$.

Question 21

For $|3x - 5| = 16$, if $(7, 0)$ and $(x, 0)$ are the two x-intercepts, what is the value of x?

Explanation

Brain/Paper Work:

The absolute value equation can be written as two separate linear equations –

$3x - 5 = 16$ and $- (3x - 5) - 16$

From the first equation, $3x = 21$ or $x = 7$ (this value is already given).

From the second equation,

$- 3x + 5 = 16$

$- 3x = 11$

$x = -\frac{11}{3}$

Answer:

Thus, the correct answer is $-\frac{11}{3}$.

A cylindrical pail has a radius of 7 inches and height of 9 inches. If there are 231 cubic inches to a gallon, approximately, how many gallons will this pail hold?

A) 2

B) 6

C) 231

D) 1386

Explanation

Brain/Paper Work:

The question requires you to apply the volume of a cylinder formula –

Volume of a cylinder = $\pi r^2 h$

where r is the radius and h is the height

$$\text{Volume} = \frac{22}{7} \times 7 \times 7 \times 9 = 1386 \text{ cubic inches}$$

Given that for 231 cubic inches, there is 1 gallon

$$\text{So, for 1386 cubic inches, the number of gallons} = \frac{1386}{231} = 6.$$

Specifics:

Choice A: incorrect because this is a result of incorrect conceptual application or calculation (this takes into account the curved surface area and calculates the number of gallons).

Choice B: correct as per the explanation.

Choice C: incorrect because this is a result of incorrect conceptual application (this incorrectly assumes that there is 1 cubic inch for every 1 gallon).

Choice D: incorrect because this is a result of incorrect conceptual application or calculation (this value is the volume of the cylinder in cubic inches, when it should be expressed in number of gallons).

Verdict:

Thus, the correct answer is Choice B.

What is the circumference of the circle in the xy-plane with equation $x^2 + y^2 - 10x + 14y - 7 = 0$?

A) 9π

B) 14π

C) 18π

D) 81π

Explanation

Brain/Paper Work:

Equation of a circle in the xy-plane takes the standard form $(x - h)^2 + (y - k)^2 = r^2$, where (h, k) is the center of the circle and r is the radius of the circle.

Now, the task is to bring the given equation into the standard form.

$x^2 + y^2 - 10x + 14y - 7 = 0$ can be written as

$(x - 5)^2 + (y + 7)^2 - 25 - 49 - 7 = 0$

$(x - 5)^2 + (y + 7)^2 = 81 = 9^2$

So, $r = 9$

Circumference $= 2\pi r = 2\pi \times 9 = 18\pi$

Specifics:

Choice A: incorrect because this is a result of incorrect conceptual application or calculation (this takes the diameter as 9, when it should be 18).

Choice B: incorrect because this is a result of incorrect conceptual application or calculation (this takes the radius as 7, the constant term in the given equation).

Choice C: correct as per the explanation.

Choice D: incorrect because this is a result of incorrect conceptual application or calculation (this value is the area of the circle because $81 = 9^2$).

Verdict:

Thus, the correct answer is Choice C.

Question 24

n years after 2012, the population of city X is given by the function $f(x) = 25000(1.05)^n$, and that of city Y is given by the function $g(x) = 40000(0.97)^n$. Which of the following accurately describes the functions $f(x)$ and $g(x)$?

A) $f(x)$ is increasing linear and $g(x)$ is decreasing linear

B) $f(x)$ is increasing exponential and $g(x)$ is decreasing linear

C) $f(x)$ is decreasing exponential and $g(x)$ is increasing exponential

D) $f(x)$ is increasing exponential and $g(x)$ is decreasing exponential

Explanation

Brain/Paper Work:

$$f(x) = 25000(1.05)^n$$

$$f(x) = 25000(1 + \frac{5}{100})^n$$

$$g(x) = 40000(0.97)^n$$

$$g(x) = 40000(1 - \frac{3}{100})^n$$

Clearly, both $f(x)$ and $g(x)$ are exponential and NOT linear.

Also, $f(x)$ is increasing and $g(x)$ is decreasing.

Specifics:

Choice A: incorrect because this is a result of incorrect conceptual application.

Choice B: incorrect because this is a result of incorrect conceptual application.

Choice C: incorrect because this is a result of incorrect conceptual application.

Choice D: correct as per the explanation.

Verdict:

Thus, the correct answer is Choice D.

Question 25

Steve lends $100 to Pat at 2 percent interest compounded annually, and uses the function $f(x) = 100(r)^n$ to calculate the total amount due to him after n years. Pat, in turn, lends the $100 to Kiran at 3 percent interest compounded annually, and uses the function $g(x) = 100(p)^n$ to calculate the total amount due to him after n years. Which of the following equations represents the relationship between r and p ?

A) $p = r + 0.01$

B) $p = r + 0.1$

C) $r = p - 1$

D) $r = p + 0.01$

Explanation

Brain/Paper Work:

This seemingly complex problem is, in fact, simple.

Note that

- the base value $100 does not change (Pat lends $100 to Kiran and not any other amount),
- the duration of lending (n years) is the same in both cases.

So, r and p can be directly related with basic arithmetic.

Pat earns 1% more (3% - 2% = 1% = 0.01) by lending the $100 to Kiran than what he pays Steve (2%).

Choice A is the answer.

Below is the mathematical understanding of the same -

Steve's $100 earns an interest of 2% compounded annually.

So, the amount that Pat should return to Steve after n years is modelled by the function

254

$$f(x) = 100(r)^n$$

$$f(x) = 100(1 + \frac{2}{100})^n$$

Note that $r \neq 2\%$. r is indicative of the resultant value of the 2% increase.

So, $r = 1.02$, and

$$f(x) = 100(1.02)^n$$

Similarly, the amount that Kiran should return to Pat after years is modelled by the function

$$g(x) = 100(p)^n$$

$$g(x) = 100(1 + \frac{3}{100})^n$$

So, $p = 1.03$, and

$$g(x) = 100(1.03)^n$$

It may be observed that $f(x) = g(x)$ when $r = p - 0.01$ or $p = r + 1\%$.

Specifics:

Choice A: correct as per the explanation.

Choice B: incorrect because this is a result of incorrect conceptual application or calculation (0.1 would be 10% and NOT 1%).

Choice C: incorrect because this is a result of incorrect conceptual application or calculation ($r = p - 1\%$ and NOT $p - 1$).

Choice D: incorrect because this is a result of incorrect conceptual application or calculation (r is clearly less than p by 1%, and NOT greater than p by 1%).

255

Verdict:

Thus, the correct answer is Choice A.

Question 26

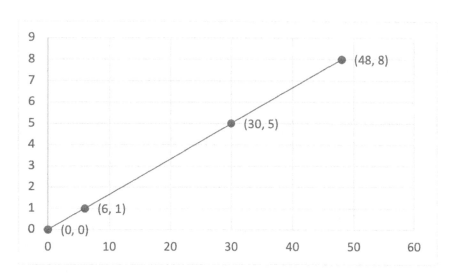

In the xy-plane, how many coordinate points with integer coordinates lie on the line joining $(0, 0)$ and $(48, 8)$, including the end-points $(0, 0)$ and $(48, 8)$?

A) 4

B) 7

C) 9

D) 49

Explanation

Brain/Paper Work:

The key to determining the correct answer for this question lies in understanding the fundamental concept that any 2 points on a straight line will have the same slope as any other 2 points on the same straight line.

The number of coordinate points with integers as coordinates will be restricted by the number of integers from 0 to 8, which is 9. Remember that the end-points also need to be taken into account!

Here, though you may be tempted to, you do not need to determine the equation of the straight line. As long as you understand that the equation of the line will NOT have a constant term (since it passes through the origin), your job is done.

So, the equation will look like $y = mx$.

Or, the y-coordinate is m times the x-coordinate.

How many such integer possibilities exist between (0, 0) and (48, 8)?

It has to be 9 (0, 1, 2, 3, 4, 5, 6, 7, 8).

Specifics:

Choice A: incorrect because this is a result of incorrect conceptual application or calculation (this takes into account only the 4 points shown in the graph).

Choice B: incorrect because this is a result of incorrect conceptual application or calculation (this excludes the end-points and takes into account only 1, 2, 3, 4, 5, 6, 7).

Choice C: correct as per the explanation.

Choice D: incorrect because this is a result of incorrect conceptual application or calculation.

Verdict:

Thus, the correct answer is Choice C.

<u>Question 27</u>

$$3x^2 - 5x + k = 0$$

In the given equation, k is an integer, and the equation has real solutions. What is the greatest possible value of k ?

Explanation

Brain/Paper Work:

$$3x^2 - 5x + k = 0$$

The solutions for

$$ax^2 + bx + c = 0$$

are

$$x = \frac{-b \pm \sqrt{b^2 - 4ac}}{2a}$$

So,

$$x = \frac{-(-5) \pm \sqrt{(-5)^2 - 4 \times 3 \times k}}{2 \times 3}$$

$$x = \frac{5 \pm \sqrt{25 - 12k}}{6}$$

It is given that the solutions to the equation are real numbers.

So, $25 - 12k \geq 0$, else the value under the square root turns negative and the solutions are no more real numbers.

Or, $12k \leq 25$

Or, $k \leq 2.0833$

So, the greatest value of k will be 2 (since k has to be an integer).

Answer:

Thus, the correct answer is 2.

A small request from the authors

If you find this book useful, your feedback encourages us and so don't forget to give feedback on Amazon.com or whatever website you have downloaded this book from.

If you want regular practice with new questions, consider visiting our website www.RRDigitalSAT.com, and register. You will enjoy the consistent journey by learning through our **SAT Question of the Day.**

ACKNOWLEDGMENTS

First of all, we, the authors, sincerely thank **YOU** for your interest in this book. This book may not be an easy one to go through, but surely is a good one to benefit from.

Creating a book with math parts is not easy. The whole credit for creating this beautiful book goes to **Damian Jackson**, of Leeds, England, who painstakingly worked on this project: www.fiverr.com/damojackson

The beautiful cover is designed by **Touhid Wahid**.

I heartfully express my gratitude to both of these creative minds.

ABOUT THE AUTHORS

Ramana Rao MLV

Ramana Rao is a seasoned educator who has been in the teaching field since 1984 and has taught more than 75 thousand students in different levels. He has taught international standardized tests for more than 25 years, landing many of his students in premier B-schools and best colleges of the world. He is the author of <u>Pearson's Sentence Correction for the GMAT®</u> published by Pearson India. He has been a senior content developer for many premier institutes in India. He is also the author of a critically acclaimed sci-fi book Heart & Brain. Currently, he is the Senior Content Developer for a premier institute in India. RR Test Prep has been his brain-child to cater to the needs of aspiring students across the globe.

Raghavender Jammalamadaka

Popularly known as RJ, Raghavender has double Master's degrees in Finance (US) and Applied Mathematics (India, Central University), international investment banking experience and a rich and multi-dimensional experience – training thousands of students over the last 20 years, developing winning curricula, expanding business – in the field of education and test prep. RJ, as Academics Head and Course Director at T.I.M.E (one of India's largest test prep companies), spear-headed academic product development (including Computer Adaptive Testing engines) and country-wide implementation. He, as National Head, Academic Operations at FIITJEE-USA Uniquest, also has rich experience working closely with high school students. His understanding and depth of knowledge about standardized tests, curricula design, top quality content creation for preparatory material, apart from his passion for exploring technology for education have aligned him with RR Test Prep.

A SMALL REQUEST FROM THE AUTHORS

If you found this book useful, your feedback encourages us and so don't forget to give feedback on Amazon.com or whatever website you have downloaded this book from.

If you want regular practice with new questions, consider visiting our website www.RRDigitalSAT.com, and register. You will enjoy the consistent journey by learning through our **SAT Question of the Day**.